HE NEVER SPOKE WITHOUT A PARABLE:
III, IV, V

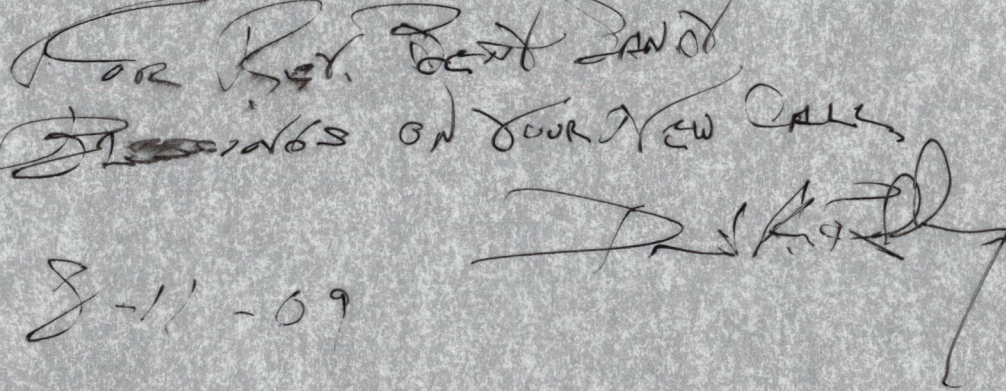

He Never Spoke without a Parable

HE NEVER SPOKE WITHOUT A PARABLE:
III, IV, V

HE NEVER SPOKE WITHOUT A PARABLE:

III. HIS KINGDOM,
IV. YOUR ANTAGONIST,
V. IT'S UP TO YOU

by David A. Redding

Starborne House

Starborne House
1262 State Route
257, South
Delaware, OH 43015
www.davidredding.com

The book cover is a painting rendered by the author's son, the Rev. David Mitchell Redding. It depicts the parable of the man who discovered a treasure in a field, and then sold everything he had to buy that field.

The author's granddaughter, Katrina Pearl Redding-Lizanich, designed the cover.

Library of Congress # Vol. 1, TX 5-759-158
Library of Congress # Vol. 2, TX 5-759-159
Library of Congress # Vols. 3-5

ISBN # 0-9671701-2-7 vol. 1, copyright 2000, Starborne House
ISBN # 0-9671701-2-5 vol. 2, copyright 2001, Starborne House
ISBN # 0-9671701-3-3 vols. 3-5, copyright 2003, Starborne House

The scanning, uploading and distribution of this book via the Internet or via any other means without the permission of the publisher is illegal and punishable by law. Please purchase only authorized editions, and do not participate in any electronic or paper piracy of copyrighted materials. Your support of the author's rights is appreciated.

Starborne House

1262 State Route 257, South

Delaware, OH 43015

www.davidredding.com

He Never Spoke without a Parable

OTHER BOOKS BY THE AUTHOR

A Rose Will Grow Anywhere	Amazed by Grace
Before You Call I Will Answer	Flagler and His Church
Getting Through the Night	God Is Up to Something
He Never Spoke without a Parable, Volumes I and II	If I Could Pray Again
	Jesus Makes Me Laugh
Liberty Beginnings	Liberty's Barn Church
Lives He Touched	Psalms of David
The Couch and the Altar	The Faith of Our Fathers
The Golden String	The Miracles of Christ
The New Immorality	The Parables He Told
The Prayers I Love	Until You Bless Me

What Is the Man?

Coming soon: Never Lose Heart (A Book of Distilled Prayers)

Jesus'
parables
make us
laugh
and cry
enough
to change
our
ways.

HE NEVER SPOKE WITHOUT A PARABLE
VOLUME THREE: HIS KINGDOM

The parables
are not
so hard
to
understand
as they
are
to do.

CONTENTS

VOLUME III – HIS KINGDOM

1. Plant Life – Matthew 13:31-32, Mark 4:30-31

    A Mustard Seed – Luke 13:18-19

    Yeast – Luke 13:20-22

2. The Buried Treasure – Matthew 13:44

    The Pearl – Matthew 13:45-47

    The Net – Matthew 13:47-51

3. The Patch – Luke 5:36

    Never Pour New Wine in an Old Skin – Matthew 13:52

4. Weeds – Matthew 13:24-31

*Any hope these volumes
have of illumining these
indispensable literary
masterpieces is due to my
beloved editor and daughter,*

Marion Telford Redding

*I dedicate them to her
with all my heart,
second,
only to the unrecognized
poetic genius
of the
Author and Finisher of
our Faith.*

David A. Redding

1.
🐾 PLANT LIFE 🐾

"God's Kingdom is as if someone scattered seed upon the ground then went to bed a few nights while the seed sprouted and grew without his having any idea how it happened. This earth produces all by itself, first leaves, then grain. All one has to do is to wait until it's ripe and then take the sickle and harvest it." Matthew 13:31-32, Mark 4:30-31

Paraphrased by the author

"My Kingdom," Jesus said, "is like nothing on earth." Still, contemporaries assumed the Messiah would fight off the Romans who were policing Palestine, and bring back the glorious reign of King David. They figured Isaiah was dreaming about a Suffering Servant, and why wouldn't Israel's Savior be somebody mounted like Caesar, commanding an army, living in a palace, and overseeing an empire?

How wrong could they be! The world has never recovered from the shock of God's surprise attack in the stable that night. Instead of a Genghis Khan, God came up with a hillbilly carpenter. His mother wrapped Him in swaddling clothes instead of ermine. It was embarrassing. Jesus wasn't dressed for it. The Kingdom of God, Jesus introduces in this opening parable, "is as if someone should plant a field then go to bed. And by the time he gets up, all he has to do is to take his sickle and harvest it." (Mark 4:26-29)

There is something for everybody to do, and at times it takes everything we have, but this parable raves about how God had it all done before we got up. Toss out a handful of seed like the baseball at the beginning of the game, then take off, and when we come back into the picture it's time to haul in the harvest. "God does it all," the parable says, "by Himself."

This parable explodes the pretensions of the "self-made man." Just because we "came to" on earth doesn't mean it's ours; hickory and coconuts fall on our heads, fish practically jump into the boat, sheep run around like a fashion parade with our coats practically ready made on them.

God cleared this place in space, manned it, sunned and rained it, got the planet going in the right direction around the sun, and even furnished the trees to keep our oxygen tank filled. What fool ever said this was man's world?

Jesus' parable proclaims that this is, and is to be, His Kingdom. We may boast colossal salaries behind half-acre desks, discuss nuclear targets and massive retaliation, but we couldn't find our way out of our backwater galaxy, even if we had the gas to do it. We don't even know what's out there multitudinous light years beyond the flickering beams of our Hubble flashlight. We are like a toddler, proud of himself for making it to the backyard fence.

Besides, we're only overnighters in this eternal motel. Even humanity's hunting phase was just a drop in the bucket of the hunt of the dinosaurs. Civilizations come and go like summer conferences. Rome's 500 years was a fast food stop compared to God's cultivation of the planet that took geological periods. "Earth produces by itself while man sleeps." "He who keeps Israel neither slumbers nor sleeps." We got in on this late, and we all have to leave early. "Thine is the Kingdom."

While we race and fret over each other's threat to our nest, it's as though the parable's declaring, God does just about everything, and nothing's going to stop Him. We could blow up the place, then He'll come in and do it right. Did a satellite the size of the moon smack the dinosaurs? "I have set before you life and death. Choose life."

A friend of mine was strolling down the street with Albert Einstein at Princeton. Einstein stopped before a tuft of grass bursting through a broken stone. He then said, "We could pave earth with cement, but sooner or later there'd be a crack, and before you know it, a blade of grass would sprout." While man sleeps or forgets, or busies himself, creation's unstoppable. This planet is going to produce, not only *by* itself, but also in spite of any opposition. Whatever it takes. God said it once, He's not going to have to say it again, *"Multiply."* "The gates of hell shall not prevail." His burgeoning seed will burst the rock rolled on top of it, just as Christ broke through His burial boulder.

David A. Redding

A MUSTARD SEED

Let me compare God's Kingdom to a mustard seed that someone planted in their garden. It grew into a tree into which the bird's built their nests. Luke 13:18-19, Mark 4:31, Matthew 17:20

Paraphrased by the author

The second parable in this trio continues the theme, "The kingdom of God is like a mustard seed, which Mark says (4:31) "is the smallest seed, which someone planted and it grew into a tree big enough for the birds to nest in."

Jesus' Kingdom is microscopic to begin with, but in the end we'll all be perched in it and flying from it, like the birds that raise their young in what came from the tiniest seed.

Stores open with lots of hype—elephants, searchlights, marching bands, enough audio to break your eardrums, prizes, coupons. Even a Billy Graham Crusade comes in pumped up with major promotion.

Not God's Kingdom. His Crown Jewel emerged remote from any palace, hidden in a donkey's feed box under a fork of hay. The priceless documents of the universe were not in code labeled "top secret." Everything was passed out such as these literary cartoons we call parables, to one child at a time.

We want to know how rich the king is, how big is his army, and how much territory is under his control. Jesus could care less. He put a child on His lap; stopped a woman from bleeding to death, and another from being stoned; spent almost all of His life in a distant rocky village; fed His crowd with a few loaves and two fish; built His church from a rough Cross, dying in the city's trash pit completely abandoned by His friends. Jesus said, "If ye have faith so much as a mustard seed, which is the smallest of all seeds…you shall say to that mountain, be moved into the middle of the sea, and it will do it." (See Matthew 17:20).

He Never Spoke without a Parable

It takes faith to believe that so little faith is needed, and I am not the only one nesting in the branches of His organization.

Some years ago my son taught me the meaning of this remarkable passage. He had a very young professor in beginning chemistry who headed up an enviable research project. Difficult as the course was, his students greatly admired the young genius for his unusual concern and compassion for them.

When it came time for their first test, the teacher was frank to confess, "Forty percent of you will not be with us after the exam because of the standards enforced by the department." My son knew that he himself would be in that 40 percent because he had gone over the material thoroughly several times and had come up with a page of key questions that he could not find the answers to anywhere in the sea of faces swimming by in that immense university. The teaching assistants appointed to help students were booked solid two weeks ahead in a vain effort to tutor a class of 400 students.

My son decided he better drop the course rather than find out what he already knew, and have it on his record. But he decided to inform the teacher personally of his decision, and to thank him. When he did the professor immediately responded, "I'll help you. You say when." "You don't understand. I have a page of questions." "Meet me at the hot-dog stand in twenty minutes." They ate and joked together, then went to the chalkboard in the empty lecture hall.

Three hours later, with the air and the young professor's hair filled with chalk dust, heartened as much as enlightened by that teacher, my son broke through his deadlocked formulae.

Realizing what a "find" he had made, and how rare such a generous person is, even among religious people, my son found himself risking one far deeper question as he got ready to leave, "Are you a believer?" "You mean, do I believe that the Son of God came to earth, died on a Cross, and rose again for us, so we could live forever?" "Yes, something like that." "No, I work with absolutes, and what you have asked is a variable."

The next day just before the exam, the student went up to the professor unable to resist one last question. "If I promise never to pester you again, may I ask you one more personal question?" "Go ahead." "Do you remember my last question to you yesterday?" "Yes." The professor was standing by the blackboard. "Do you have just a drop of that faith I spoke to you about?" The lecture hall was empty. The professor looked away, turning the

David A. Redding

eraser in his hand. It suddenly got very heavy. No one before had ever exercised such artistry on the young professor. He was compelled for the first time to think this variable through. Finally he said, "Yes, I do. I don't think I could go on living unless I had a drop of that faith." And somehow a great load was lifted from that student and moved into the sea that day for that professor. "If ye had faith as a grain of mustard seed."

 YEAST

The Kingdom of God is also like yeast, or leaven, which a woman hid in three measures of dough until it was all raised.
Luke 13:20-22

Paraphrased by the author

Jesus' third parable also reinforces this concept of God's mighty empire coming out of infinitesimal origins, "The Kingdom is like yeast which a woman hid in a massive amount of dough until it is raised incredibly." (Luke 13:20) Not only is a pinch of leaven, or yeast, also little, it doesn't make any noise, recalling Elijah who didn't find God in the storm or earthquake, but in a cave in "a still small voice." We mistakenly sing, "Like a mighty army moves the church of God." Instead, it moves like light. God did not announce His favorite Son with the head aching din of a political convention. He did it with a star.

The King of Kings was born in secrecy and slipped up on mankind in unprepossessing sandals. There was no thunder of hooves, or twenty-one gun salute, no squadron piercing the sound barrier overhead, no chatter of drums. "Every knee shall bow" in silent confession. "Be still and know that I am God."

We will not hear His guns at Armageddon. He will take us without firing a shot. As Sir John Seely said, in his magnificent life of Christ, *Ecce Homo,* in describing the building of the new Jerusalem, "No man heard the clink of trowel or pick axe; it descended (silently) out of heaven from God." "The Kingdom is like leaven."

"The Kingdom is like leaven which a woman hid in an enormous amount of dough until it raised all of it." The Kingdom is not like unused yeast, but yeast that works its magic invisibly and overnight. Christ is taking over, not by a *coup d'état* but by infiltration, not political, nor academic, but atmospheric. "Not by might, nor by power, but by My Spirit, says the Lord." (Zephaniah: 4-6)

"Until it was all leavened." Andrew affected Simon Peter, Philip found Nathaniel, and the dying Stephen ignited Saul who was watching Stephen martyred instead of watching the coats, and on and on it goes. Until *much* is leavened? No, until it is *all* leavened. God's not a quitter; not content with a few good men and women, making a hierarchy of heaven itself. Just as farmer God is not going to suffer a crop failure on planet earth, so this image of the yeast lends itself to a thorough redemption of creation — "Until it was all leavened."

"The light shines in the darkness, and the darkness {can never} overcome it." Standing beside the graves each of us must take heart, for "no one shall snatch you out of My hand." "Not one of these little ones shall perish." Our God is not only the author, He is the finisher of our faith, and will never give up until the last enemy is destroyed and the last lost sheep is found.

There was a time when even Christ Himself assumed He was sent only to the lost sheep of the house of Israel, but the Syrophoenician woman whose daughter He brought back to health, the Roman Centurion whose serving boy He healed, to say nothing of Greek Luke and the Pharisee St. Paul, made clear that the Gentiles are included. All were obnoxious to the self-righteous as were the women who trailed Him, along with the unemployed riff raff. How long it has taken us to realize that black slaves were in on this too. And, finally at long last, we're grasping that His company includes losers. He shared death row that day with a criminal He took with Him. At the last minute He rescued a prostitute, condemning those about to cast her out forever, saying, "Is there no one left to accuse you?" "No one, Lord." "Neither do I. Go and sin no more."

Do you know of anyone from whom He withheld the leaven? "In Christ there is neither slave nor Greek, Jew or Gentile, male or female," saint or sinner. All are one to Him. The Kingdom is like a woman who hid enough leaven to raise the whole world until it was all raised.

David A. Redding

2.

 THE BURIED TREASURE

Then too, Heaven's Kingdom is like someone finding treasure buried in a field, and because of his joy, he sold everything he had to buy that field. Matthew 13:44

Paraphrased by the author

he Kingdom," Jesus said, "is as if someone found buried treasure, and in his joy he hid it, and sold everything to buy the field where it was."¹ We have picked paradise apart until nothing's left but rubber chickens and some harp plucking, but Jesus highlights it as the hidden treasure worth everything we have.

His stories are like magnets. His Kingdom starts like a tiny mustard seed, and then works as quietly as bread rising, and as C. S. Lewis put it, you are *Surprised by Joy*. It is as if some trespasser trips over the corner of a chest sticking out of the ground filled with gold. Burial was safer than banks in those days. Did you become a believer like that?

For centuries churches have taken joining up very seriously, certainly not in the profit column but in the loss column. Sunday morning wives drag husbands off the golf course; mothers threaten teens with youth group. They haven't found the treasure yet. Christ is too good to be true, and when He happens to you, Sunday will outshine Saturday night and make the lottery look sick.

Most of us preachers don't look as though we'd found anything to shout about except

---

¹ *The Gospel of Thomas,* which made it into the Apocalypse, but not into the Bible, muddies the crystal clear meaning and confirms the wisdom of the canonizers. According to Thomas, "A man had a treasure in his field and didn't know it. His son inherited the field and sold it without knowing about the treasure either, and the man who later plowed it up lent it out at interest."

He Never Spoke without a Parable

how bad off you are and how hot it's going to be. But this parable's about your ship coming in. For all we know, this fellow cutting across that field didn't have a thought in his head, didn't have a prayer, deserved to be locked up. Out of the blue, seemingly apropos of nothing, God's grace hit him upside the head, and he was wealthy beyond belief. Jesus' Kingdom does afford a time to pray, a time to cry, but as a friend is carving on his own tombstone, also a time to yell "whoopee!"

Our time has gone mad wanting to be millionaires. We may have sawed off the last leg of Long John Silver into a fast food fish house, but he was Robert Louis Stevenson's famous pirate in Captain Flint's *Treasure Island*. Charles Dickens takes Pip finally to his *Great Expectations*. And, what an Olympian piece of deep sea exploration there has been recently about the treasure ship of all time still being raised off our east coast where it sank in the gold rush.

We're closer to the foot of the rainbow than we think. Somehow the Bible is the treasure map, far more reliable than Captain Flint's with far more at stake than we suspect. Jesus is telling this story of buried treasure to us to save our souls.

I remember the exact spot in my boyhood where I discovered buried treasure. I too was out standing in a field. It changed my whole life far more wonderfully than had I won four aces. This was treasure Jesus had buried for me.

Grade school had been hell for me. I remember every single elementary teacher as my enemy, so you can guess who was at fault. Miss Mitchell, my third grade teacher, made sure everyone realized she was highly thought of by telling them she had never failed with a child. I was sent to break her. Her weapon was standing behind the third grader and shaking him. The desks were bolted to the floor. I learned the trick of hanging so tightly to the desk that her teeth rattled. My desk was still loose when I checked years later. Finally, after I put my parents through innumerable humiliating conferences in the principal's office, Miss Mitchell conceded she had failed with me.

I would never have burned down the school, though I wouldn't have cried if it had. I just battered it mainly by inattentiveness, sitting in the back row, staring out the window, and waiting for the bell to ring. Teachers let me pass only so they wouldn't have to put up with me for another year.

My dad softened my rebellion by buying a remote farm in the hills of eastern Ohio. He said it was for his health, but I knew it was also to get me off the streets. Going home

David A. Redding

on the last day of school my freshman year, I knew for sure I'd flunked. The other kids were yelling to each other, "What'd you get in Algebra? How about science?" My grade card was still in the envelope unopened. Everybody knew my standing so nobody asked me.

After I got off the bus and started up the lane I finally pulled out the card to face the damages. Seventy-five was failing — Algebra, 74; Science, 76; English, 75. I tossed it on the dining room table. My parents handled me right. They never said a word. Somehow they knew to let go and let me work it out on my own with the One in charge.

I worked hard that summer behind the Percherons, my dog never leaving my side, and I loved every minute of it. Late that summer, standing there in the field, I remember the exact spot, I also realized that Someone was watching over me, and suddenly I found myself talking to Him about my life. It got very heavy and before I walked away, I told Him that the coming year there'd be no more sitting in the back row staring out the window and waiting for the bell to ring. I'd sit in the front row and write down every single thing the teacher said and give it everything I had.

At the end of the first six weeks grading period there I was again sitting on the bus listening to the yelling, "What did you get in Plain Geometry? How about Ancient History?" But I was too bruised from my past record to reach into my pocket and see how I fared in front of everyone. Besides, I shuddered that even after all my effort I might still not have what it takes. So, I waited until I got off the bus and started up the lane, then I stopped.

I pulled the card out of the envelope. The sun was shining. I can see that card as plainly now as then, Plain Geometry, 97; Ancient History, 98; English Literaature, 96. Then my eyes blurred over until I couldn't see any more. I felt the joy of the man in Jesus' story who had stumbled on buried treasure. And while I continued to work hard and tried not to stare out the window, I still have a long way to go before I can say, "I sold all that I owned to buy that field." But since that time no one's been able to talk me out of the One who left me the treasure. And I know it has to do with much more than good grades.

THE PEARL

Also, the kingdom of Heaven is like a buyer after expensive pearls, who when he found his most fabulous pearl, he sold everything he owned to buy it. Matthew 13:45-47

Paraphrased by the author

I wasn't looking for God. He came to me when I was looking for a way out. But Jesus told another parable about a merchant who was actually searching for good pearls and ran across the pearl of all time. The first man fell into the treasure. It was pure grace, no effort, but the pearl merchant had long had his eye out for the best pearl. It was not a surprise, so much as a triumph.

Pearls were highly prized back then, bringing big business to divers in the nearby Persian Gulf or Red Sea. Cleopatra wore a pearl worth 100 million sisterces, roughly 2 million pounds sterling before recent inflation. And Matthew, tax collector that he was, did not miss Jesus being correct in perceiving what people coveted.

The last part of this tiny story reinforces the former one. The pearl merchant invested all he had to purchase the pearl of a lifetime, just as the finder of the treasure sold everything he owned to get the field where the treasure was.

You can't have Christ without loving Him body, mind and soul, as the Great Commandment demands. Other god's have to go, money, glory, control, credit. "No man can serve two masters." A push and a shove won't do it. Ten percent won't do it. It takes nothing less than everything. The find is so infinite, it embarrasses the most that anyone can do. Both finders couldn't wait to spend their last dime on their discovery.

You will remember the story of the pearl diver whose father sent him down too deep for the big ones. The son finally surfaced, his fist tightly clenched over an enormous pearl, but it had taken his life, somehow symbolizing the way the Apostles died. Can't you imagine them opening St. Peter's fist after he was crucified. Surely his heart contained, if not his hand, the pearl of great price.

Selling everything we have to buy the field, or afford the pearl, doesn't mean we have

David A. Redding

an auction, give it to the church to share with the poor, then with the last thousand sail to serve in Africa. Jesus did recommend that as an individual prescription to someone where money had replaced God. But the Bible does not say that "money is the root of all evil." It says, "The love of money is the root of all evil." God doesn't want us to resign, just let Him be the boss, put our stock in Him. Like Christ, we too must be about our Father's business. It doesn't matter how much Bill Gates has, it's whether he realizes he's employed.

    When I thought about what example I would use where someone had thrown in with God, I thought of the lovely Miranda in Shakespeare's play, *The Tempest*. She and her father, the magician, Prospero, had been shipwrecked on an island. Now a young woman, she had never seen a man other than her ancient father. In *The Tempest*, the ship of the young prince, Orlando, is wrecked, and he is no sooner ashore than she falls in love at first sight and says, as you'll remember from tenth grade English, "O brave new world that has such beauteous creatures in it." Soon she said the line every man yearns to hear. Miranda blurts out, "Oh, sir, I'll be your wife, if not, I'll be your mistress, or if not, I'll be your slave." Miranda actually proposed to Orlando as all of us should propose to God, as these two stories suggest in buying the field or selling everything off to get the pearl.

    The joy of the treasure and the pearl come when we give in and give it all up to God. It belongs to Him. We belong to Him. And we'll be amazed how easy a taskmaster He is as compared to money, or a wife with her hands on her hips, or an irate husband with the veins swelling on his forehead. This is the big deal Christ sanctions. Sign up. Birth certificate II. All out to God. It's where the joy is that goes on and on.

 THE NET

Again, the Kingdom of Heaven is like a net flung into the sea. When it was full they drew it ashore, filling jars with the good catch and throwing the rest away. That's just like the end of the world when the angels will sever the bad from the good, casting them into the furnace of fire where there shall be wailing and gnashing of teeth. Matthew 13:47-51

Paraphrased by the author

The last little story that tags on this trio is called the net. The version in the non-canonical *Gospel of Thomas,* chapter 8, repeats a similar theme, "A smart fisherman cast his net and caught a big one, so he threw the small ones back." When someone catches on to the Good News, the rest of his catch is valueless. However, Matthew records how Jesus slants this same parable into judgment day. After the net is hauled in, the fishermen go through the catch throwing out the culls. Instead of the joy the finders had in trading everything for the treasure and the pearl, this features the dark side. His angels pitch out the joyless ones in the end.

     Jesus doesn't treat us like vegetables. We were handed an extremely important life. This isn't a dry run. We work better, as Charlie Brown said, under pressure, and tomorrow there will be lots of pressure. We must not take God's mercy lightly, nor His warnings with a knowing smile. God will not be taken lightly. The parables include Jesus' saying, "He who has ears to hear, let him hear."

David A. Redding

3
 **THE PATCH**

Then He told them this parable. No one ever cuts a piece from new cloth to patch a worn out coat, for it will look as bad as before. Luke 5:36

Paraphrased by the author

The Pharisees were harassing Jesus long before they sicced the Romans on Him to hang Him on the Cross. This time when they condemned Him He told this parable. They taunted, "Why don't your disciples fast like John the Baptist's?" This was really damning Him, "Why don't you do things the way they've always been done?" Change was anathema to those religious wardens.

Jesus was a jolt. Pharisees didn't have to follow Jesus around very long to realize He was never going to fit in their square hole. The only fast Moses demanded was Yom Kippur, the Day of Atonement, but fasts had multiplied like flies until the Pharisee in Jesus' parable boasted, "I fast twice a week." Religion had gotten so bogged down with added restrictions that a woman could not look in the mirror on the Sabbath for fear she would see a gray hair and pull it out. This was the excess weight Jesus was so busy jettisoning that they feared it would turn their world upside down.

When the old religious security guard accused Jesus for not fasting, He did not retaliate. He came up with a perfect answer on their terms, "My operation is like a wedding." Pharisees had practically turned worship into a funeral. Jesus was celebrating God as the Father of the Bride, not our taskmaster. Jesus said, "How can you force my followers to fast, when the Bridegroom hasn't left yet?" Jesus identified Himself, not as a pallbearer, but as a Bridegroom, the image of joy and festivity.

Then Jesus told this parable of the patch so everybody would know He was not adding on one more Jewish sect; He was ringing church bells. It went like this, "No one ever patches an old coat with a piece of new cloth or it will tear a worse hole."

Christ rolls up the cosmos here like an old coat, and unrolls the new cosmos like a new one as in Hebrews 8:5 and Psalm 102. His concept is new yet with familiar imagery. Also, in Acts Peter dreamed of a sheet lowered from Heaven bulging with every kind of creature convincing Peter that everything was eatable, kosher or not. The Gentiles could come in, not just the Jews. The old skin's out, the new wine skin's in.

Jesus also feared His inflammable faith would shred the old. Christianity must wear a new coat or split it's Father's down the back. The Talmud was too set in its way to be revised, too delicate to take the strain of the youngster He was setting loose.

Today, across this country we hear the old fabric tearing. The mainline denominations are in grave danger of splitting apart. Methodists are torn into factions. Will the old robes hold? Episcopalians have been ordaining conservative Bishops despite rigidly liberal dioceses. President Thomas Gillespie of Princeton Theological Seminary, has predicted that Presbyterians are headed soon for division.

Here's how it is. When we lived in St. Augustine, Florida, before we moved back to Ohio, the High School Young Life Campaign got going with a bang. One hundred and fifty kids were meeting each week in private homes. There was lots of laughter, as kids lives were turning around from drugs to Christ. It was not a deadly church youth group. It was on fire. Kids were being saved. It was like an old-fashioned tent meeting with current sophistication. Joy raised the roof. You could hear youth singing for a block in the unchurched suburbs. And there were a few dune buggies parked on neighbor's flowerbeds.

And what literally amazed me was that all this fresh spiritual excitement that was attracting the youth, was resented by conventional church-goers. Finally, a local policeman picking up on that prejudice said, "Ain't that many kids meeting each week for nuthin.' It must be drugs. It sure ain't church." And they raided us, which you can imagine brought kids on the run as far away as Jacksonville. Naturally, other churches, struggling to maintain a youth group, resented such an enormously successful all church, one having so much fun, trusting their Bibles, and making a buddy of Christ. Such excitement had long fallen out of favor among the intellectuals.

David A. Redding

That nearly broke the wineskin. Their two famous converts were Booger & Smiley, and Rev. Smiley started a new Presbyterian church in St. Augustine.i[2]

Now we here at Liberty Church haven't yet enjoyed a police raid. However, its growth and laughter has been difficult for our sister churches to understand. Like the police in St. Augustine, they assume it can't be God; they tend to be suspicious.

Our sister churches are dying. Fifty churches a week have been dying in this country for almost fifty years. So they've got to believe growing churches must be some throwback of religious red necks. Most of our mainline churches only have about 100 members. Our big downtown churches are shadows of their former selves. To them we're not funny, we're odd, and off.

It's as though we're not fasting either. Too much Bridegroom, not enough funeral. Singing crazy contemporary songs. "Why don't you have a pipe organ? Why are all those young folks there?" No pipes, strings. We're not perfect. I pray to God we're not obnoxious. Truly live churches don't get fan mail from a dying denomination.

Three summers ago a traditional Episcopalian noticed his congregation was getting older, and there were more and more empty pews. So, the *Atlantic Monthly* sent him across the country to find why some non-mainline churches were beginning to grow fantastically. In Charles Trueheart's article in *The Atlantic Monthly* "Welcome to the Next Church,"[3] many new churches seem to have found the fountain of New Wine of which Jesus spoke.

 # NEVER POUR NEW WINE

IN AN OLD SKIN

Jesus explained," Every legalist who is converted to

---

[2] See the chapter on "Two Wild Ones" in the author's *A Rose Will Grow Anywhere*.
[3] "Welcome to the Next Church," Trueheart, Charles. *The Atlantic Monthly*; Aug 1996; 278, 2; ProQuest Direct Complete, pg. 37.

Heaven's Kingdom is like someone who brings out new and old things from his treasures." Matthew 13:52

Paraphrased by the author

The final parable in this trio appreciates the old and the new. It goes something like this, "Everybody who has been trained for the Kingdom of Heaven is like a resident who brings out of his treasures both old and new things." Jesus used soap on the past, not acid. The New Testament quotes much of the Old. And Jesus is concerned about His Good News as well as His Father's faith, so He also tells the story's twin, "And no one puts new wine into old wineskins, for the new wine will burst the skins and spill it." You will never be able to pour the Gospel into the Torah without ruining both. Judaism had come to mean monastic caution, a mad competition in restraint among archaic Elders. Jesus was adding a big room. Joy takes more room than a new wing. Frail B.C. could never cradle virile A.D.

This parable, particularly, lends itself to a wide spectrum of applications. Think of how it applies to our own personal conversion. Most of us come to church to get a shot in the arm, when we need a complete overhaul. I'd appreciate a band-aid or two this morning, but God would like to restore me. I'd like a sip or two of the new wine, to mix with the old. No, He wants to empty me out and pop me into a new container." Remember the song from the musical, *For Heaven's Sake*, "I asked God in to make a few repairs, but He's making the whole place over."

A new believer may need a new building. He may need to stop going to the old bar and stay away from those guys who never went to bed and never had a thought in their head about God. A recently cleaned heart can pick up grime off the walls associated with the way they used to be. Better throw that old picture book away, get unglued from those "soaps." Is playing that much Bridge doing that much for me? God bless the synagogue, but Jesus would have torn it up. He needs a cathedral or two. "Where two or three are together in my name, I'll be there too."

What about you and me? Can we patch our present job, or friendship? Or should we find another? One woman told me if she had known what leaving her drunken husband was going to do to her children, she would never have divorced, come hell or high water.

David A. Redding

And yet I have approved divorces before the situation deteriorated to crime. We have more bewildering options today, but let's avoid spilling any more of the new wine. We must not worship church. We must not worship our will, our way. We must worship Christ.

In the 1500's Martin Luther and the Pope called each other the Anti-Christ. Luther thought the people were worshipping the Pope, and the Pope thought Luther worshipped the Bible. The old wineskin split down the middle and a lot of wine was spilled. Luther tried to patch it up by nailing 95 complaints on the church door, but the Pope threw him out and Luther put the fresh wine in a new wineskin. There were faults on both sides, in many ways a sad story. Our Liberty Church is as much of a bridge as there is, putting Catholics and Protestants back together. But just as Jesus was thrown out of the synagogue so Protestants were thrown out of the Roman church, and it had to do with new patches not working on old cloth, and spilling wine all over the place.

I came via Columbia University, and Vanderbilt from a liberal background, my wife from a devout conservative one. So when her parents first heard me preach, they wept; and it was not from inspiration. Soon after, they sent us a copy of the official Thompson indexed King James. I needed it. I'd been taught a lot about God, and about the Bible, but my wife and my in-laws, along with my mother, drew me to God, changing me until I dedicated my book to them, *The Miracles of Christ,* which Harper & Row even reprinted. Talk about treasures old and new, a classmate wrote me, "Dave, I read your new book and was appalled. Did you forget everything you learned in seminary?" And that is the typical viewpoint of properly credentialed ministers. Charles Trueheart found some old treasures among his new churches as we have at Liberty. While there's lots of applause, tears, and laughter, no neckties, and strings, there's a return to God. The "live" churches have rediscovered the electricity of the Bible, and that making friends with Jesus can "jump start" someone such a dramatic way that traditional churches might find naïve, if not objectionable. We hope that our Church, like the live flourishing ones that author Trueheart found, is less inhibited by ordained personnel, really demonstrating the priesthood of all believers, and a meltdown of the too-defensive denominational stance.

The children from the church school were all sitting quietly on the floor in front of me at a recent church service. I asked them, "What did Jesus ever do for you?" One little three-and-one-half year old girl raised her hand, came up to my lapel mike, turned around to face everybody and said, "Jesus brought my mommy back to me." It was the kind of statement back in my liberal heyday when I would say, "That's very interesting." Now, with others, I wept, convicted in my deepest heart there is something more going on in church than a self-improvement program. Could it be, as I'm coming to believe, the resurrection of the dead?

David A. Redding

 WEEDS

The Kingdom of Heaven is also like a planter who sowed good seed in his field. Then while everyone was asleep an enemy sowed weeds and disappeared. So the weeds came up along with the crop. Then the field hands asked, "Do you want us to pull the weeds?" "No," the owner replied, "for while weeding you might uproot the wheat. Let both grow together, till harvest time, then I will tell the reapers to bundle up the weeds and burn them, but haul the wheat into my barns.

Jesus then left the crowds and went into the house where the disciples asked him to explain the parable about the weeds. Jesus answered, "I am the Sower." "The field is the world." "The good seeds are my children, the weeds are children of the devil who sowed them. The harvest is the end of the world, and the reapers are angels. And just as the weeds were burned, so the angels will collect all the obstacles and destroyers to be burned where there shall be weeping and gnashing of teeth."
Matthew 13:24-31, 36-44

Paraphrased by the author

he Kingdom of Heaven is as though somebody had sowed good seed in his field, but that night an enemy sowed weeds and got away with it.

This enemy, like some peeved neighbor back in ancient Palestine, was never caught. Somehow, after a great start Creation had a bad night. Geologists are preoccupied with how long it took; Jesus studied how to fix what went wrong. Genesis mentioned a snake in the garden; Jesus detected bad seed.

Just as the good seed shot up and produced practically all by itself in another of His parables, so here a common poisonous fungus sprouts. *Lolium Temulentum,* called darnal, looks like wheat,[4] and can riddle the field, without much help from poor farming practices. In the parable the weeds were planted by the enemy, and the tragedy here doesn't seem to be our fault anymore than we can take credit for fat figs and giant walnuts.

Every acre of our field is choked with this fake flax, downtown and country, on and off campus, both sides of the tracks. It's creeping up the aisle of the most magnificent cathedral. In *The Confessions of St. Augustine,* you discover even saints have dirty thoughts. You even will find treason cropping up among the Twelve Disciples.

This parable must have been heartbreaking for Christ to tell on God. Being about His Father's business was not uncomplicated. This story confides that Heaven's highest hopes had been blasted and Jesus' work was remedial. James Russell Lowell told of a painting he saw of an angel holding back God's hand as He was about to launch another such susceptible planet as earth.

The parable of the tares is almost an apology. Evil is not in your imagination; an unsuspected opponent slipped the seed into the field and it somehow slipped by God. It's still virulent, after the best that Christ could do, so far. While many do fancy the Devil too much, we really do have an enemy who has contaminated the crop, and we're stuck with it. Whatever we do now is remedial.

Some of us came from a dysfunctional family, some of us are working on one, some of us have detected a yellow streak not on our X-Ray, and some of us see red all the time.

Don't blame God. "An enemy did it." This is a mouthful. "Every good and perfect gift cometh from above." "In Him is no darkness at all." God is the Maker of Heaven and Earth, not Hell, not the headache earth gives us. Hell is God's very absence, not something He makes.

So this nearly perfect crime is not quite the whodunit of all time, for Jesus exonerates God just as Moses did. And you cannot blame it all on humans either. This disaster is far beyond the scope of the worst of us.

---

[4] Found in a 4000 year old tomb in Egypt (Zohary p.161) quoted in *The Parables of Jesus,* David Wentham, Intervarsity Press, 1989, p.75.

David A. Redding

Volcanoes were belching lava on the poor mammoths eons before Adam ever arrived, and if a gigantic satellite smacked the dinosaurs long before we got around to blackening lungs with tobacco, livers with cirrhosis, mowing each other down in such numbers on the highways, and making war a minor sport, we are only accomplices. Our shoulders are only so broad. We are supposed to accelerate the Day when the lion and the lamb can cuddle up, but we had little to do with the conflict in the first place. "An enemy did it."

What are we going to do about it? Are we going to let these blighters get away? The servants asked the owner, "Would you like us to tear out the tares?" We could shoot some evil people down, and put up more penitentiaries. Then again, that would only leave a scorched earth. These servants are thinking about purging the church rolls, getting rid of dead wood, engaging in one heck of a witch hunt, activating the Inquisition with more red hot forks and pokers, instead of looking at themselves.

God sent Jesus to scope this strategy out, and Jesus' parable opposes instant zapping of the evildoers. "If you tear out the tares now, you will uproot the wheat." You can't tell the difference between wheat and these weeds early on. Besides, even if you could, their roots are already so hopelessly intertwined, you'll never pull up one without damaging the other. Our weeding would ruin the crop. And we might miss our own weedy reflection in the mirror. Let God do it later.

Repeatedly Jesus declares, as He does in John 3:17, "I came not to condemn the world but to save it." So don't be in such a hurry. The Devil's already doomed, and if he's embarrassed Heaven and bloodied us, he's only delayed His own destiny.

Jesus sees through our predicament. Pulling a bad tooth can jeopardize its neighbor. An electrocution affects the electrocutioners, just as brainwashing and illegal interrogations boomerang. Getting rid of a criminal may break his mother's heart as well as those who feel he's innocent, or believe he's had an authentic change of heart. These weed pulling contests aren't what they're cracked up to be. And as Aleksandr Solzhenitsyn, in *The Gulag Archipelago*, warns us, "If only there were evil people somewhere insidiously committing evil deeds, and it were necessary only to separate them from the rest of us and destroy them. But the line dividing good and evil cuts through the heart of every human being. And who is willing to destroy a piece of his own heart?"[5]

---

[5] *The Gulag Archipelago*, p. 103, {NY: Harper & Row, 1975}.

One cannot tell with people, even more than with crops, how they're going to turn out in the end. A well-curved ball doesn't look like a strike to the umpire until it's practically in the catcher's mitt, so he judges it at the end of its trajectory. Many juvenile delinquents, like St. Augustine, turn into saints. Prodigals do come home and Eagle Scouts tragically jump off buildings. Who are those busy compulsively deciding who's going to Heaven and who's to be burned? (see Genesis 13:15).

According to Christ's story, God declares, "Leave it to me!" Who would ever have picked the disciples? But God said that impetuous Peter would pull through, doubting Thomas would get over it, and that whore Mary Magdalene was going to turn into a blessed angel. Poisoning rats you risk your dog, and weasels are too smart to eat D-Con; they'll keep on cleaning out the hen house. No, God said, "Let wheat and weeds both grow side by side until harvest, and at harvest time I will tell the reapers to gather the weeds first and tie them in bundles to be burned, but collect the wheat for my granary." This parable was also true to Palestinian rural life back then, for they bound the "fool's wheat for fuel."

Not too long ago one of my son's teachers from junior high stopped me in the supermarket. She had had him in class during his most challenging years. She had felt he had no potential, so as she asked me about all our family, I knew she was working her way toward asking about one particular son. She wanted to see if her negative evaluation was justified, and she was savoring already hearing that she was right.

So, when she asked, "And n_____?" I answered, "He's in arctic Alaska." That didn't surprise her, so she probed, "But what's he doing?" Determined to make this paternal triumph last as long as I could, I stalled. "He's working in a hospital." Hoping still to confirm that her grim prophecy had been fulfilled, she pushed me to the wall. "I mean what is his *position*?" I said somewhat sadly, thinking of her, "He's a physician." She smiled and said, still incredulous, "No, no, I mean n_____!" As she shuffled off, I noticed she was not whistling. "Let them both grow side by side until harvest and at harvest time I will instruct the reapers."

While Matthew goes on to explain how the fruitful wheat will shine like the sun while the barren burnables wail to the accompaniment of gnashing teeth, I must confess how difficult this subject is for me. I matriculated at a seminary that had trouble believing in heaven, let alone hell. It is much easier to take hell lightly when it is only referred to indirectly in the Bible, but hell is vibrantly woven into the very fabric of one of Jesus' major

David A. Redding

stories.

While I was attending this "tolerant" seminary, I fell for my fourth cousin. I hadn't seen her since she was in pigtails, and I went head-first. She was, I might have known, attending a perfectly proper Presbyterian seminary that left no doubt in any one's mind that sure enough there was too a hot fire waiting. And since our schools were 1000 miles apart, we had to carry on by mail. And wouldn't you know, our main topic gravitated to whether there was a Hell. How we got engaged, I don't know. (Well, yes, I do but I won't go into that.)

I couldn't believe how a just God could put any of us away forever in the pit of fire just for a short life of petty crime. Before she knew it hell came between us. Hell had a big place in her Bible, and she went to her favorite theology professor to see if she should break up with me. I always tease her that he told her that he thought we should get married, and that that would take care of it. And it was so. After a few years of married life I was able to embrace this elusive theological concept! The truth is, as you suspect, she taught me instead about Heaven.

Seriously, I have come to respect God's final audit; He's bolder than Santa Claus. He can be blunt. I've suspected that those who defended Hell most fiercely, intend it for others, but the Great Commandment is not only a choice. It has teeth. God's not going to shanghai anyone into Heaven or Hell. You volunteer. You're asking for it.

This parable kills the idea of reincarnation. Who would ever take this life seriously if they always have another chance? Wheat is not a perennial. Someone quipped, "I used to believe in reincarnation in my former life, but then I was born again."

Far more ominous it would be if God never did make the crooked straight and left the dissonant note of cracked Creation forever in the air, never resolved. How inconceivable to leave God merely the Author and never the Finisher of our faith. None of us will ever get away with the murder in their hearts; neither will the Devil ever get away with it. This isn't an unfinished symphony. How good of God to be definite.

How kind it was of Him to announce the final exam so far in advance, "And at harvest time I will tell the reapers."

Jesus'
parables
make us
laugh
and cry
enough
to change
our
ways.

HE NEVER SPOKE WITHOUT A PARABLE
VOLUME FOUR: YOUR ANTAGONIST

The parables
are not
so hard
to
understand
as they
are
to do.

He Never Spoke without a Parable

CONTENTS

VOLUME IV – YOUR ANTAGONIST

1. Are You Coming To Dinner or Not? – Luke 14:16-24 –

   Matthew 22:1-14

2. Two Debtors – Luke 7:36-50

   Two Creditors – Matthew – 18:21

3. The Barren Fig – Luke 13:6-9

   The Line of Duty – Luke 17:7-1

4. The Man God Called a Fool – Luke 12:13-21

David A. Redding

 ARE YOU COMING TO DINNER, OR NOT?

A man invited a large number to supper, even sent out his servant to tell them when it was ready. However, every single one of them excused themselves. The first explained, "I must go look over the field I bought." Another said, "I must inspect five pairs of oxen I recently purchased." Another reported, "I have just been married, so you will realize I cannot come." These excuses infuriated the master, so he ordered his servant, "Go out immediately into the streets and back alleys of the city and get the poor, the sick, the handicapped, and the blind to come to my dinner." The servant reported back, "There is still room for more." So the master declared, "Go up the highways and into the brush until we have a full house. None of those I invited earlier shall get a taste of my banquet." Luke 14:16-24

Paraphrased by the author

The Kingdom of Heaven is like a king who planned a marriage feast for his son. He sent out his servants to invite the guests but no one would come. So, he sent out other servants to tell everybody that supper was ready. The oxen and fatlings are butchered. However, they all sneered; one went to his field, another to his business. Others seized the king's servants, insulting and killing them. This infuriated the king, and he sent his army to burn their city and destroy them. Then he told his

David A. Redding

servants that the feast was ready but those invited were unworthy. "So, go out the main roads and invite anybody you can find." So they filled the wedding hall with good and bad. When the king entered, he noticed one guest who was not dressed for the occasion. And when the man offered no excuse, he had him bound and thrown into the darkness where there shall be weeping and gnashing teeth, "for many are invited but few are picked." Matthew 22:1-14

Paraphrased by the author

king once invited practically everybody to a fabulous wedding banquet for his son. It was not just any king, or superman, as Matthew tells it. It's another parable about God. In Luke's version it is not a king, but a rich man. God has invited us to dinner. He's not just our Creator; He's our Host. This time we're not servants, we're guests. This is how Jesus photographs His Father. Picture God pondering the options at Creation. Mover and Shaker that God is, a glance above at night tells you there's not a lazy bone in God's body. The Hubble scope confirms the Creator's still sprinkling the frontier of the cosmos with stars. However, the job wasn't enough; God wanted company. The Maker pulled relatives out of the dirt, and all inherited God's jaw.

Jesus could have presented God with a spear, eager to lead us hunting in a massacre of the mammoths. Or why not imagine God as a slaveholder like Simon Legree? Jesus could have dressed God up as Hagar the Horrible, as though we were all still sweating it out on death row. Jesus could have caricatured God as some kind of red faced engineer, shoveling us like fuel into Lucifer's runaway locomotive, or wrapped our Maker in the imperial toga of a Caligula sacrificing us for entertainment, as well as feeding the king of beasts, in a bigger and bloodier coliseum. Instead, God changed the bad news, as it must have appeared, late that fateful night in Sodom and Gomorrah, into Good News. What did God do? He invited us all to dinner. He wanted us sitting with Him around the Table at the rehearsal dinner for His Son.

This parable is better than Genesis! Jesus began with a Table instead of a Garden. Hawaii would be nice. Disney World's not bad, but huge salaries and an overnight to Mars, fall flat beside the wonder of the wedding of The King of Heaven.

We are fascinated by the art of the banquet. P.G. Wodehouse, Britain's pope of farce, actually detailed a duke's twelve-course blowout during the heyday of Queen Victoria. A world-renowned cardiologist left heart surgery for a long vacation, so he could study cooking in Paris at the *Cordon Bleu*. One gourmet there dined alone on a $4,000.00 meal, and lived to tell about it. Earth's head spinning banquet took place not long after General Eisenhower was President. Our librarian looked it up for me in the larger than *Life Magazine* pages. It was put on by the last Shah of Iran to celebrate the 2500th anniversary of the founding of his Persian Empire. It was held in the glorious ruins of the palace of Persepolis where the unconquerable Cyrus had ruled.

The Shah of Iran blew gold like water to decorate those towering pillars lingering in the remote desert to make ready for the guest. It included the Queen of England, the Pope's High Cardinal, the Vice President of the U.S. and his wife, Dukes, Premiers, and most honored of all, that picturesque Lion of Ethiopia, Haile Selasse.

Each Monarch had their own tent in this 200-acre spread with finger touch control to lower the 102 degree daily temperature and raise it from 28 degrees at night. A million was spent on colored lights to paint the evening desert.

The menu for this cream of society included quail eggs, roast peacock, raw camel, and **Château Lafite-Rothschild**, 1945, all flown in from Maxim's. Yet this was only a fast food carry out compared to what God's cooking up for us. The Bible says, "Nobody's ever seen, or heard of, or even guessed in the wildest imagination of his heart, what God is fixing for supper."[1]

Guess the response to Jesus' royal invitation? According to Jesus' story, nobody showed up. "They all alike began to make excuses." This story's not about 2000 years ago. Jesus told this on us, too. We may say grace and take a communion crumb but we never really mix it up around the table with Jesus. We can't remember a word He said to us during the meal, or what it was like sitting beside Him.

---

[1] 1 Corinthians 2:9 But as it is written: "Eye has not seen, nor ear heard, Nor have entered into the heart of man The things which God has prepared for those who love Him." (NKJV)

David A. Redding

You'd think we'd give our eye teeth to rub shoulders with Jesus, share His dessert, pick up some of His animation. No, we don't get that close. Our prayers are canned, the second verse is the same as the first. We go to church, but we're not all there, as we are at the fifty yard line, or into the ear of the love of our life. Saints may say that they cannot wait for the Rapture, but when it comes right down to it, we're not ready. We're like the congregation at the prairie revival, singing their heads off about how they couldn't wait to get to Heaven, but when the cowboy at the back took out his guns and shouted, "Now, everybody who wants to go to Heaven stand up!" No one stood. Only St. Paul rose to the occasion, "For I am hard-pressed between the two, having a desire to depart and be with Christ, which is far better."[2]

Jesus took the wind out of all our huffing and puffing about Heaven. We have shriveled Heaven into perching on a cloud and strumming on a harp alone, secretly suspecting with Mark Twain, "Heaven for climate. Hell for society." Who envies the dead?

A supposedly "twice born" man once wrote Billy Graham about whether he would have to live with his earthly wife for eternity. He could handle a 1,000 years, but eternity?

Narrow little minds have helped to ruin the ecstasy of what the last book in the Bible calls, "the wedding supper of the Lamb." (Revelation 9:9) We lost the Garden, and now we're *under* the Table, instead of getting caught up in the celebration.

You'd have thought scalpers would be making a killing outside the king's banquet hall. No, Jesus reported three typical R.S.V.P.'s.

"The first said to Him, " I have bought a field and must go look at it." Who could believe this? Anyone would look at a field, *before* he bought it. It's not only a flimsy excuse; it's a joke. He not only rejects Heaven for a cotton patch; he ridicules it. He was too arrogant to sit down and eat with God.

No wonder Jesus requires us to become like kids, for adults think suspiciously. A child trusts, imaginatively. Adults scorn, "I have to look at my field." The devil has bent us into eating like horses, standing around and gulping it down; this speed trap keeps us from the benefits of togetherness, and we avoid getting to the essential things. Rushing around we'll

---

[2] Philippians 1:23, NKJV.

be less likely to let the secret out, the one that opens the door to each other and to God. If we can create the time to come to Supper, He'll make it well worth our while. "Where two or three are gathered in my name, I am there too."

The second excuse is also bigoted and absurd. "I have bought five pairs of oxen, and I must examine them." Jesus doesn't miss the irony of someone waiting to inspect oxen for which he's already paid. No farmer would risk that much without checking first. His excuse also boasts ten oxen which loudly cries how important he is to be plowing about ten thousand miles.

Our own excuses are just as preposterous. God wants to bring home the succulent bacon and pass far more than the butter to us, but we can't see it. "We've just got to wash our socks." How did Jesus know whether to laugh or cry?

The third excuse was, "I just married, so you know I'll never make it." There's no "Please excuse me." You can't be all bad if you are doing what your wife wants. Wrong. We're responsible to Someone higher than *Better Homes and Gardens."* You can ignore God in church, or home, work or the golf course as well as in Las Vegas. What makes the difference whether you are playing cards or giving to charity? The point is, "Are you coming Home to dinner or not?"

What upset the king was that they didn't want to be with him. He had his servants beat the bushes for guests from the ghettos, out of vexation, not kindness. He was furious at their refusing Him, but it is certainly the way anyone would feel about such frigid shoulders.

The parable reveals the whole world's reaction to God's invitation. Just as John says at the beginning of His gospel. "He made the world and moved in, but His people would have nothing to do with Him. They wouldn't let him in. They wouldn't come near Him."[3]

Freud and Marx scorned this forever "eating" at the church as though food was not necessary for life, so church nutrition has the quality of a hospital menu. "Get it over with and get on with the book review." No! Disciples could have fasted His last night. No! Gone over test questions. No! They dined out later in the Upper Room, and they did not

---

[3] John 1:10.

David A. Redding

even recognize Jesus until they were eating his bread together. He fed five thousand in all four Gospels, plus another four thousand in Matthew and Mark. His first miracle was not a healing, not even a prayer. He simply furnished an enormous quantity of expensive wine. What Jesus wanted was to show us the sacred thing that only happens to us around the Table, the wonder of what we express to each other back and forth with Him, in the most enjoyable domestic setting.

He truly is our bread and wine, and the other food that's beyond us, to say nothing of the water that makes us never to thirst again. "I am,"[4] He said, "the Living Bread."[5] "Our fathers all had manna but they died, but {His} food's for good."[6]

A king once gave a wedding feast for his son, and invited practically everybody. And when a straggler finally barged in dressed only in disrespect the king bounced him. He insulted the king by attending callously, as the others had been cruel by their absence.

The last honest literary critic in the Soviet Union, the editor of *Novi Mir,* was the first to read Alexander Solzhenitsyn's, *One Day in the Life of Ivan Denisovitch*, the book that made Khrushchev weep Russia into the thaw of communism. The critic read the first page in bed, then got up immediately, dressed in his tuxedo, and all alone read the great classic sitting ramrod straight in a proper wedding garment.

In one way I come to Him *"Just As I Am,"* but in another respect, it had better be in "my Sunday best."

---

[4] Exodus. 3:14.
[5] John 6:51.
[6] John 6:49.

TWO DEBTORS

A Pharisee invited Jesus to dinner. Jesus no sooner came into the house and reclined than a sinful woman entered with an alabaster jar of expensive perfume. She stood behind him weeping on his feet, kissing them, and wiping them with her hair. Then she anointed them with her perfume. When his host saw it, he said to himself, "If this Jesus were a prophet he would never have let this sinful woman touch him.

Jesus read Simon and said, "A creditor had two debtors. One owed five hundred 'dollars' and the other fifty. Since they had nothing to pay he forgave them both. Which one will be most grateful?" Simon answered, "The one to whom he forgave more." Jesus answered, "Right."

Then Jesus asked Simon, "Do you see this woman? I entered your house and you did not even give me water for my feet, but she washed them with her tears and wiped them with her hair. You did not greet me with a kiss, but she never stopped kissing my feet. You did not anoint my head with oil, but she anointed my feet with perfume. So, her many sins are forgiven because she loved much, but he to whom little is forgiven, loves little." And Jesus said to her, "Your sins are forgiven." The other guests murmured, "Who does he think he is, to forgive sins?" But Jesus said to the woman, "Your faith has saved you. Go in peace." Luke 7:36-50

Paraphrased by the author

David A. Redding

ne time a prominent Pharisee named Simon had Jesus over for dinner, more for amusement, than for inspiration, never guessing that he was asking for it. Jesus no sooner reclined to dine as they did in those days, than a spectacular "call girl" crashed the party. Upper class dwelling in those days often opened off the street, so passersby might sit in the entryway, although it would be unthinkable for lepers and prostitutes. So, Simon was mute with fury at the intrusion of this "woman of the night."[7]

Before Simon could have her thrown out she had started something that would find its way into the New Testament, and be remembered forever. She suddenly knelt behind Jesus and broke open an alabaster jar of expensive perfume, probably her life's savings, as well as for cosmetics to conduct her profession. Weeping she let down her hair, something a woman never did in front of anyone but her husband; she covered His feet with kisses, and washed them in the perfume. Maybe she had already heard Jesus, still amazed at the Grace that had saved a wretch like her. Perhaps she had trailed Jesus there to sob out her sins, pour out her new happiness, and publicly give her whole heart to the Lord of her lost life. Hebrew, Aramaic and Syriac have no word for thanks, so she erupts with it. This was a night she would not have to forget and would help her forget the others. How could anyone who ever heard about the table that was spread that night ever forget?

If Simon was incensed about such a woman barging into his dining room, he was absolutely fit to be tied over his dishonored guest's misbehavior. He said to himself, "If this man were a prophet he would know right off what sort of woman this is who is practically seducing Him in front of us.

Jesus read Simon's mind and quickly set him straight. "Simon, do you want to know something?" "What's that, Reverend?" Simon's tone, no doubt, accentuated his scorn. Certainly the woman had been rapidly learning that there was far more to her new Lord than one could expect from the usual hermit from the hills. She had every reason to fear that Jesus would turn His back on her for getting Him thrown out, particularly when He already had enough enemies to nail him. She was finding far more to Him than goodness.

---

[7] The other reports of the story of the perfume do not include the parable: Matthew 26:1-13 and Mark 14:3-10. Scholars dispute whether they are variations of a different story. I think that is a futile fussing.

He wasn't easily intimidated. Here Jesus is under fire for public disgrace hardly helpful to His image of Messiah. It had never occurred to this woman that she had just engaged a magnificent trial lawyer that both of them suddenly needed. In moments He developed a brilliant case for their defense that Socrates himself could not have matched. It was this parable.

It was the case of a prostitute versus a Pharisee. "Two men," Jesus began, "owed money to a loan shark. One owed him five talents and the other fifty. Unbelievably, he forgave them both, now which will love (thank) him more?" Simon was cornered. He had to answer, "I guess the one for whom he forgave more." Jesus did not accuse Simon. He let him hang himself. One of the Gospel's breakthroughs came just then out of the mouth of that fossilized Pharisee who wouldn't forgive his dog.

Then Jesus let that Mephistopheles of religion have it:

> Simon, do you see who this woman really is? When I entered your house you insulted me by not offering me the customary water to wash my feet, to say nothing of seeing that your servant did it. But as soon as she came in, she began washing My feet with her tears and wiping them with her hair. It is as though you set out to humiliate Me, for you didn't extend the usual courtesy of a kiss, but she hasn't stopped kissing My feet. You did not bother to anoint My head with the traditional oil, while she has done it with expensive perfume.
>
> I tell you, Simon, though she painted the town red, she's forgiven, for her thanks has opened her heart. You wouldn't know what to do with forgiveness. She sees and suffers from all that's wrong with her. You can't see how you've ever done anything wrong because you've never cared that much for anybody.

Then Jesus turned to the woman, "All is forgiven." Jesus did not turn to Simon. This doesn't mean Jesus took her sins casually, and He doesn't mean that the more you sin the more forgiveness you'll receive indefinitely, or the more you'll thank God for it. Remember

David A. Redding

the Devil dared Jesus to leap off the pinnacle to show off God's maximum grace, but Jesus answered, "Thou shalt not tempt the Lord thy God."[8] Jesus is complimenting this woman for confessing how far she'd gone wrong, and appreciating what a King's helping of mercy it took to save her from herself. He is waiting for each of us to make that life-giving discovery of Him for ourselves.

Simon assumed there was nothing wrong with him, like the smug goats in Jesus' last parable. Simon had no use for a Savior, nor for anyone else. Jesus called such bigots "blind leaders of the blind." They could not see how the harlots and outlaws would not only beat them into Heaven, but they might not even make it themselves; for while Pharisees obeyed the rules, they were heartless.

 TWO CREDITORS

"How many times should I forgive," Peter asked Jesus, "if my brother keeps on doing me wrong? Is seven times enough?" Jesus answered, "No it should be seventy times seven." Think of the Kingdom of Heaven like this. There was once a king who decided to settle up with his staff. The first man's debt ran into the millions. Since he could not possible pay it to meet the debt, the king ordered him, his wife, and children, to be sold, along with everything he had. The man fell face down at the king's feet and begged him, "Give me some time, and I will pay everything back." The king's heart went out to him, he freed him, and cancelled his debt.

But the man no sooner got out than he ran into a colleague

---

[8] Matthew 4:7.

who owed him a small amount. He grabbed him by the throat and growled, "Pay me what you owe." The man fell face down at his feet and begged him, "Give me some time, and I will pay you." But he refused and had the man thrown in prison until the debt was paid. Others were so upset they told the king. The king was so enraged he had the man brought in, "You scoundrel. I cancelled your debt when you begged me as you should have done to your debtor." The king ordered the man tortured until he should pay up. And that is how my Father will treat you unless each one of you forgives your brother from your heart. Matthew 18:21-25

Paraphrased by the author

This second parable of forgiveness is introduced when Peter asked Jesus, "How many times do you have to forgive somebody who keeps doing you wrong? Peter volunteered tentatively, "I don't know whether I am up to the daunting ideal of seven times." Who but Peter would have aimed so unreasonably high? Who could ever bring himself not to hold it against someone who kept knocking him down over and over again? I would feel as though I deserved the Congressional Medal of Honor if I succeeded in actually forgiving somebody once. Seven times? Dream on. No doubt Peter assumed he'd outdone himself by suggesting seven. The disciples must have shaken their heads again over Peter's impetuosity, just as later in Upper Room when Jesus had offered to wash Peter's feet, Peter had finally replied, "Better bathe me!"

Jesus' answer to the question, "how often we should forgive?" is still mind boggling! He shot back, "No, not seven times, I tell you, but seventy times seven." This is more difficult to believe than the resurrection. For if you are planning on Heaven, unrestricted forgiveness comes first. You can break commandments and still get in, but you'll never get in so long as you leave anyone unforgiven.

As the disciples were standing around stupefied by this bombshell, Jesus came up with this story, "Here's the way Heaven is. One time a king was settling accounts with his staff. The first man up owed an almost inconceivable sum, 100 million *denary*. Since there was no

David A. Redding

way under the sun he could pay it back, the king ordered him to be sold along with everything he had; that auction block included his wife and children, certainly abhorrent, but a common practice then among gentiles in the Middle East. It doesn't say whether he squandered, lost, or embezzled it. He owed it. Now he had to pay for it in a fate worse that death. However, even his and his family's slavery would not come close to raising the cost of what he owed.

No wonder the man fell prostrate at the king's feet. "Please be patient, and I will pay it all back." That was a promise only Midas could have kept. Somehow, even though the king surely smiled, he was so moved with pity he forgave the official his entire debt.

You would think that such a royal gesture would have broken that sinner's heart wide open to God, but he no sooner left the throne room than he grabbed a little fellow by the throat that owed him only 100 *denarii*, a piddling amount compared to the mountainous debt the king had just forgiven him. But he threw the little guy in jail, despite similar cries for patience.

This upset the colleagues of the cruel official so much they told the king about it. The king roared with rage and hauled him in. "You scoundrel! Here I cancelled your enormous debt when you begged me, even rescuing you and your family from slavery, and now you've thrown your poor victim into prison who only owed you a trifling sum. Then the king condemned the man to torture until he paid it off. Jesus wrapped it all up by a warning to us, "God will do this to you too *unless* you forgive your brother from your heart."

We mistakenly think we can pack Heaven with decent, law-abiding folk. No! Heaven's filled with the forgiving. Hell bulges, not with bad guys, so much as with those who still have it "*in*" for someone. If you meet someone in Hell you'll find he's still holding something against someone. Repentance is the door to God. The best of us are the most ashamed. It was perfect St. Francis of Assisi who said, "Nowhere is there a more miserable sinner than I." "All we like sheep," the Bible says, "have gone astray." We need forgiveness as desperately as the dying man who is crawling and clawing his way toward his nitroglycerin. Recognition of our own need to ask forgiveness may even be the first step to offering forgiveness to someone who has hurt us. We need to take that step, not just for our own sanity, but to unlock the door to paradise.

We need to choke out, "Forgive me!" and to say, "I forgive you!" not merely as a courtesy, but from our toes, as that prostrate debtor begged in his emergency. Christ died for our sins, but that's not enough. We must forgive those who've sinned against us. Jesus said so.

More mandatory than commandments are Jesus' ultimatums, "Unless you become like a little child you cannot enter . . . " "You must forgive your brother from your heart or I won't forgive you." Even forgiveness is not enough; we must become a forgiving person. I suppose we could still be touchy, still get mad, but we can't hold a grudge. Forgiveness is expensive, but is fruitful. It's pure joy!

Homesick for Ohio and its four seasons, and also hoping that a change would be good particularly for our four teenagers, I agreed to accept a call to Liberty Church. We dreamed of moving to Sky Farm along the Scioto River, building a stone house with our own hands, and raising beef cattle.

It seemed so idyllic a plan that I sweetened many a social evening boasting of our ambitions, fully believing that such a prospect was a modest goal for so talented and unified a family as ours; three big teenage boys, my wife, daughter, and me. We had no better sense, nor humility, than to announce it in advance on our Christmas card.

Everyone worked furiously the first few days on what I thought was the tool shed. It turned out to be the music shack. After that burst of energy everything went wrong. I had forgotten all about the mud in Ohio. The summer swam by in a sea of futile exertion. By August when we had planned to be under roof, we were still mired in the foundation, money running out, winter coming on. Another parable burned deeper into my soul, "This man began to build, and was not able to finish."[9]

House plans never show how enormous a project would prove to be to amateurs. Then the black day came when someone left the garden hose on to pack the fill dirt behind the longest masonry wall thrown up since the Great Wall of China. The hose did settle the fill dirt, but the wall fell over. It had not cured sufficiently to take such pressure.

The natives had been restless for some time, but we all became so devastated by this catastrophe, and realized how poorly skilled and inexperienced we were for such an

---

[9] Luke 14:30

David A. Redding

extensive effort, that we were reduced to fighting shamelessly among ourselves. I am grateful to this day that no tapes have surfaced.

One of the members of our family was a perfectionist and the rest of us just clods, so the drama of our conflict developed between him and the rest of us. I don't know who opened fire the day the long wall collapsed, but my perfectionist son was into it with the other two boys so fiercely that they headed toward the opposite corner of the disaster area to lay down their tools and hitchhike back home to Florida. The house building was all a voluntary effort, and they were old enough that they were free to go.

And as the dreams for our building the house together went up in smoke, I climbed into the argument against the perfectionist too. I had been trained by experts. My mother and father had fought before me and taught me everything I know. My father had been an Appalachian athlete with very little academic background – so fought as with a great broadsword, making mammoth strokes that missed. My mother was from upstate New York, the sixth generation in the same house. She had taught in college. She fought with words as with a rapier, never missing, until by the end of the evening my father stood, drawn, in his doorway, figuratively, covered with "blood." But he always came through with this strong finish. He would wait for my mother to catch her breath, then he'd sigh, "All right, Mother, forgive me for living," then immediately slam his door.

Finally my son called me a name I could not believe he would call his own father, my being a minister and all. With my early domestic training, I knew exactly what to fire back, but for some reason I couldn't speak. Perhaps it was because the other boys were about to leave and the tragedy of our dream breaking up took the heart out of me. I found myself saying instead, "Son, you really know how to hurt a fellow." It was the best thing I ever said.

Everything got quiet and when I looked up I saw my perfectionist son tapping on his wall with a trowel. There were no tears, but I could tell from his face that he was weeping. The other boys saw it too, and we were all suddenly at his side.

Many of us are glib with words. Others of us, often it's the perfectionist, don't say things easily, so when they speak it means something. We were completely unprepared when he said, "I hope you all will forgive me for treating you like '------,'" and he used a one-syllable word. We could not believe our ears. He was wearing a red New Holland farm

He Never Spoke without a Parable

equipment cap. He reached up, took it off, and looked up. "O God, I hope you'll forgive me for treating the ones I love best like '------,'" and again he used the one-syllable word. Then we were in each other's arms.

That put us back in business building the house. Visitors say, "It must have taken a lot of work to build this house." We did work hard, but what built the house was someone's having the courage to say, "I'm sorry," and others swiftly responding, "It's OK."

For the first time I understood the meaning of the Scripture, "Except the Lord build the house they labor in vain…"(Psalms 127:1). One cannot build a house, or keep a son, or hold any home or planet together very long without forgiveness.

Shylock, in Shakespeare's play *Merchant of Venice*, wanted justice, a pound of flesh, in return for his pound of gold. Portia, in her role of Doctor of Laws, told him off forever with these memorable words:

> The quality of mercy is not strain'd;
> It droppeth as the gentle rain from heaven
> Upon the place beneath. It is twice blest:
> It blesseth him that gives and him that takes.
> 'Tis mightiest in the mightiest; it becomes
> The throned monarch better than his crown;
> His sceptre shows the force of temporal power,
> The attribute to awe and majesty,
> Wherein doth sit the dread and fear of kings;
> But mercy is above this sceptred sway,
> It is enthroned in the hearts of kings,
> It is an attribute to God himself;
> And earthly power doth then show likest God's
> When mercy seasons justice. Therefore, Jew,
> Though justice be thy plea, consider this-
> That in the course of justice none of us
> Should see salvation; we do pray for mercy,
> And that same prayer doth teach us all to render
> The deeds of mercy.

David A. Redding

3

 THE BARREN FIG

A man had a fig tree planted in his vineyard, and he waited in vain for it to bear. So, he told his servant, "This fig has not born for three years, it's wasting space. Cut it down." But the servant said, "Let's give it another year. I will fertilize and cultivate it, then if it still doesn't bear you can cut it down."
Luke 13:6-9

Paraphrased by the author

 THE LINE OF DUTY

Suppose one of you has a servant plowing or minding sheep. When he comes in from the fields will his master say, "Sit down and relax?" Won't he say instead, "When you have finished preparing and serving my supper, you can have yours." So it is with you all. Until you have finished your work for the day you should say, "We deserve no credit for only doing our duty."
Luke 17:7-10

Paraphrased by the author

Insurance Policies still call disasters an act of God, just as busy bodies back then expected Jesus to assume that about Pilate's massacres. Jesus shocked them with his sharp objection! No! Those fatalities were no worse sinners than the rest of us. "You will all end up like that unless you repent."

Jesus went on, "Do you think that those eighteen Israelites on whom the Tower of Siloam fell got what they deserved anymore than everybody else in Jerusalem? Unless you're sorry and have a change of heart you'll end up the same way."

Jesus was trying to break down "stuck up" hypocrites like me. There's no such thing as an innocent bystander! We are no better than those who got on the plane that went down. Only bigots condescend to casualties. Jesus was taking the weatherman down a peg. No tornado ever twists through town so as to slam the damned and avoid those with good Sunday school attendance records. This conversation introduces Jesus' parable, "A man had a fig tree planted in his vineyard," a common practice then, though this reminds us that God had carefully planted Israel in his earthen vineyard with unique expectations.

The only tree mentioned in the Garden of Eden is the fig tree. It is the Bible's favorite. It's leaves furnished the first "ready to wear." We might fantasize our ideal throne as a deck chair on a Caribbean luxury liner beside the bonbons and tropically flavored beverages, but an Israelite pictured himself, "under his fig tree, under whose shade you cannot be scared." (Micah 4:4) And the fig tree is unusually appropriate for Jesus' purposes. Like no other tree it blossoms inside the fruit itself and the fig tree bears almost all year long. Curse the fig tree and you curse Israel "dead on it's feet."

Then the owner instructed his caretaker, "Chop that worthless shrub down. I haven't found any fruit on it for the last three years." The point to life is production. It's not whether someone was blown up or washed away but whether he came through with why he was born. Rachael and Hannah were dying to have kids but "barren" involves far more than being childless.

A person cannot confess his faith adequately with his lips. "By their fruits ye shall know them." We are not Christians because we say we are, but by whether we are fertile. We give ourselves away by our fruit just as a tree does.

How would you prove you were a Methodist? Providing a picture of yourself in the

David A. Redding

third row of your congregation would not do it. Sometimes people think they're good Presbyterians just because they believe in Predestination, or because they know the subject cold. Jesus shot down all those answers with this parable. To prove we are believers will take evidence. Reading the Bible and praying doesn't go far enough. What do we have to show for it? What fruit has my faith yielded?

It has been good form since the twenties to cut down great men. Writers have long been whittling away at Washington and Lincoln. How tragic we cannot say anything nice about Henry Ford now without being laughed out of class, yet we're picking up the fruit still falling from his tree. Two more industrial tycoons we've torn to ribbons as "Robber Barons," but we're still living on their "produce," John D. Rockefeller and his partner Henry Morrison Flagler.

The church I served in St. Augustine was built by Flagler for his beloved daughter. He and his wife are also buried there. Flagler's desk had been next to Rockefeller's in Cleveland. Rockefeller said Flagler came up with the idea for Standard Oil. Flagler and Rockefeller were not only unbelievably generous, they gave to God. Both of them were daily Bible readers, known for their praying. Both of them still bear fruit; they are like olive trees that bear forever.

The Titan confirms Rockefeller had far more money than anyone else ever had, taking inflation into account Rockefeller gave far more libraries than Carnegie but wouldn't let them use his name.

Flagler left for Florida for his wife's health, then built the railroad from Jacksonville to Key West that the interstate now uses. They wanted to call Miami, Flagler, but he wouldn't let them. He built the beautiful Methodist church in St. Augustine as well as the Cathedral of North Florida which Dee and I served almost ten years. Thousands of tourists visit it weekly.

Our greatest preacher, Harry Emerson Fosdick, refused John D. Rockefeller, Jr.'s offer of a church for fear of Rockefeller control, but Rockefeller promised and built Hudson's Riverside Church that got Broadway through two world wars. Fosdick was my pulpit hero and his book on *The Meaning of Prayer* is still the masterwork on the subject.

The fantastic United Nation's building did not come from the government. It was the fruit of John D. Rockefeller Jr., who managed the family's magnificent stewardship. They were guilty of the sins of their time, but rose farther above them than we have from ours. It wasn't just that banks bounced when Rockefeller wrote these checks, it was the fruit Christ was talking about still as fresh as the Golden Delicious at the supermarket preserved from the orchard last fall. I am overwhelmed by the brilliance of Rockefeller's bounty every time I visit Williamsburg. Williamsburg is an answer to prayer without preaching. Every brick of those disintegrating historic buildings was numbered and put back in it's place, to give us back the authentic rooms, for instance, in Chowning's Tavern, where Washington and Jefferson dined on the same Brunswick stew and Scuppernong wine, as Pilgrims are now served with the same Elizabethan accent, by attendants in the authentic knee britches or the gowns that reach the floor of our cherished patriots, calling the Fathers of our country back to mind. You can sit exactly in Patrick Henry's pew or stand where he said, "I know not what others may think, and if this be treason, make the most of it, but give me Liberty or give me death."

No university professor, nor politician, ever cherished this memory enough to restore this Holy place. It was Rockefeller. You've got to go there. See the film first. Stay at the lodge. See the shops of the cooper, the leather, the hat, harness, cabinet, pill and wig maker, and hear the colonial militia firing, and have your Christian experience there which our government has since forbidden in it's buildings. I'll never forget the guide at the House of Burgesses treasuring the gift of God Williamsburg is by quoting founding Father, George Mason, when he was asked not long before he died, "What was it like as our country was being born?" He paused, and overcome with emotion he said, "It seemed as though we had been treading on enchanted ground."

You'll come away from Williamsburg realizing you're carrying away more than baskets of fruit. That town was planted in God, The Father Almighty, and in Jesus Christ His only Son our Lord. And can you believe that that charity that Rockefeller gave to all of us has become one of the most fabulous business successes in the world.

The most impressive legacy Flagler left, and he had less than 200 million to give Florida, a pocketful a century ago, was the Ponce De Leon luxury hotel like no other in all the world. It was the Disney World then. Before the Titanic took him down John Jacob Astor, and the presidents in or out of his pocket stayed there then along with any kings and queens who sailed over here. Palm Beach then was still a beach, Naples nothing but a stable

David A. Redding

for boats and horses.

That historic hotel whose Spanish spires you still see in the distance in St. Augustine, closed the year my family arrived at the church across the street, and I count it among my most exciting experiences to have had a part in it's rebirth as Flagler College, where I taught and received my most treasured degree. It's restoration has been done as meticulously as at Williamsburg. Now it turns away more student applications than the Ivy League schools with its new state of the art multi-million dollar library. So many other bequests lavished on the past have long since been dead, dried, and buried in memorials or museums, as much of St Augustine was before this college. Flagler bore fruit.

Flagler College features whom I presume to call my dear friend. Founding president, Bill Proctor, has not only tied the school to the nation's most creative deaf and blind facility where my wife, Dee taught, but also to the Christian program of the Young Life Campaign that changed the town. Flagler hit St. Augustine like a constructive tornado. He still is bearing fruit through others grafted to the Spirit.

You and I may not bear fruit of that magnitude, but we can hoe around the trees and sing about it, and one can pray all our energy won't go to leaves. And if we're planted in God's Holy Word and given to Christ, we'll grow a green thumb. The caretaker in this parable talks the owner into giving the barren tree another year to get it into production, and while the manure and cultivation don't do it for this doomed tree, this second chance is promising for us.

Some of us do feel half dead, dried up, and could do with more than irrigation, or the "miracle grow" that comes from being near Him who even changed water into wine. We know that somebody can memorize the Bible, and display a chest covered with church attending records, but still be sterile. We must, as the Sacrament of Baptism declares, be "grafted onto Christ."

The thrust of Jesus' parables comes nearer home than Israel, or the "almost chosen people," as someone named America, or even the celebrities of stewardship. How are your figs? Our "good deeds" don't qualify as fruit, necessarily. We can give to outwit the I.R.S., or to strengthen our dossier, but that's no yield from our true nature. A poor basketball player can have a good night, but you can expect it from a good one. You can tie on some good deeds like expensive ornaments on a cut Christmas tree, but that's not fruit. "By their fruits ye shall know them." "Do they gather grapes from thorns, or figs from thistles?" (Matthew 7:16) "A good tree cannot bear evil fruit." "Every tree that doesn't bear good fruit is hewn." (Matthew 7:18) Until we are grafted onto Christ, we are not going to yield what we're born for, "I am the vine" he said, "ye are the branches."

Pharisees acted like the cat's eyebrows because they were meticulous keepers of the rules. But Jesus jerked their chain hard with the parable in Luke 7:7-10. Almost everyone with anything had a servant in those days, often hiring out their child to be one. And the servant received no bonus for doing what was expected of him. Plowing and cooking was just carrying out orders. Pharisees acted like Almighty God just doing what they were supposed to do. It was fruitless. They were like trees only looking after themselves. "We deserve no credit for what's expected." The purpose of life is beyond the line of duty. It is what you offer others that becomes you. "Oh, that's just like her."

David A. Redding

4
THE MAN GOD CALLED A FOOL

Someone from the crowd shouted, "Teacher, tell my brother to split the inheritance with me." Jesus replied, "Who appointed me to divide it up?" Then Jesus explained to his disciples, "Watch out for covetousness, because life does not depend on how much you get." Then Jesus told this parable. "A rich farmer was wondering where to store his bumper crops. 'Here's what I will do. I will tear down my barns and build bigger ones to store the surplus. Then I will tell myself, "You have enough for so many years, take it easy, eat it up, drink it down, enjoy."' But God replied, 'You fool! This night your life will be demanded of you. Now who will get all you left behind?' That's the way it is for someone who lays away treasures for himself and is not rich toward God." Luke 12:13-21

Paraphrased by the author

omeone from the crowd collared Jesus, "Rabbi, force my brother to divide up the inheritance with me." You can tell what Jesus thought of this by his answer. Who appointed me to divide this up? The man did not say, "We're quarreling, please referee." He just told Jesus, "Fix it," and of course in his favor; the Middle East was forever fuming over real estate by families, if not by nations.

Jesus' job, however, was to get us to *give*, not get. Jesus was never into "rights," but into doing the right thing. Remember the two mothers who came to Solomon, each claiming the same baby. He solved it by deciding to divide the baby in half, revealing the true mother by her tearfully surrendering her rights to save her little one.

Taking sides so often leads to bloodshed; our Civil War was also a dispute between brothers that cost more young American lives than all our other wars. Dr. Kenneth Bailey remembers that this was what turned Shakespeare's *Romeo and Juliet* into a tragedy, such as our Appalachian feud between the Hatfield's and the McCoy's.[10]

In *Romeo and Juliet* Tybolt kills Mercutio, then Romeo kills Tybolt, so Lady Capulet demands the death of Juliet's beloved Romeo, wrenching this sob from the prince:

> Where be these enemies? Capulet, Montage,
>
> See what a scourge is laid upon your hate,
>
> That heaven finds means to kill your joys with love!
>
> And I, for winking at you, discords too,
>
> Have lost a brace of kinsmen. All are punish'd.[11]

The brother in the parable not only admits he's fighting with his brother; he wants to finish him off. He doesn't want a brother. He wants what his brother's got.

The inheritance doesn't matter that much to Jesus. What matters is his brother. This is the only time this Greek word for "divider" is ever used in the Bible, "*Meristes.*" If we drop the "r" and move the "i" and the word becomes "*Mesites,*" which means, "reconciler." Jesus' native Aramaic introduced Luke's word play, which the same passage in the *Gospel of Thomas* leads one to favor the translation, "O man, who made me a divider?" In the *Gospel of Thomas* it is rendered, "He turned to His disciples and said to them, 'I am not a divider, am I?'"[12]

Jesus scolds this quarrelsome brother, "Watch out for covetousness. Your life is not what you have." This obsession with acquisition is like being squeezed by an octopus, strangling our laughter, our love, and all the music in us. Don't fear robbery, or even your brother's stinginess, what's going to get us is our own greed.

We can carry mace, even a shoulder pistol, and install the most sophisticated security

---

[10] Bailey, Kenneth E., *Poet and Peasant through Peasant Eyes*. Erdmann's, Grand Rapids, Michigan, Copyright, 1976.
[11] Shakespeare, *Romeo and Juliet*, Act V, Scene 3)
[12] Aland, 526, quoted in <u>Ibid</u>, *Through Peasant Eyes*.

David A. Redding

system, but we have met the enemy and it is us. What is stealing us blind is our own selfishness.

Then Jesus told this jarring story. "A rich man was having such incredibly heavy harvests, he didn't know what to do with it all." A wise man would have figured out how his bumper crop was a loan, not a gift from God, to include others, as Joseph used his surplus to solve famine in Egypt.

However, this self-centered fellow reads his receipts as booty. "I'm the master of my fate and the captain of my soul." As Scott says, He "mismanages the miracle." He doesn't see God's name on his windfall. He doesn't belong to God. God's not in on it, so he's grabbed God's seat, and talks to himself about what to do. Joseph reserved his fat years for others, but this lottery winner squirrels away the loot for himself.

The man doesn't say that he's merely adding storage space, "I will tear down my barns and build huge warehouses." He almost sounds like he's building vaults, not only to make room, but for keeps, for he goes on, "Dear me, (meaning 'dearest me') I've got enough piled up here for myself until the end of time, so Soul, we are not only going to take it easy, we are going to live it up! So, "eat, drink, and be merry."

This lucky sport worships pleasure like the Epicurean named Sarainaplus, who put it this way, "Eat, drink, and sport with love, there's nothing else, if the dead don't rise." What else is there, if there's no tomorrow?

Without a divine Governor, one never goes to bed, one never gets up. We're out of control and pulled apart by centrifugal pleasures. There's no one to keep school. School's out! We're made to be disciple, disciplined, managed. The captain is no sooner off the ship than the crew's drunk on the medicinal brandy, like a completely unchaperoned fraternity house, "They'll never catch us. What have we got to lose?"

Bailey points up another play on a Greek word. It's translated into English as "enjoy yourself," but the Greek adds the prefix *"eu"* for intensity, *"euphero," "euphron,"* our way of saying, "a hot time in the old town tonight." *Phero* enters our English language as *diaphram*.

Then God thunders into this bedlam," You fool!" And out of the four Greek words for "fool," he selects the word, "*Aphron*" (mindless), which plays on the word, "*Eupheron*," which is used here for "living it up."[13]

"You fool, your soul is required of you tonight." And the Greek word used for, "required," is the same one used to call in a loan.[14] The "fool" had fooled himself into thinking he was "a self-made man." He regarded his harvest, not even as good luck; it was all to his credit. Nothing could have been further from his empty head than that he was under any obligation.

God goes on, "And now who will get all your storage bins?" The announcement of his execution that night probably shook him up too much to think of writing a will, but God's making him think of the afterlife for the first time. "Securities" was the wrong word for his holdings. More than a rug had been pulled from under him.

This parable, as with all of His parables, is told to all of us. Who is going to get what we are working on? It doesn't mean pension plans are mistaken. Just don't stop there. Is writing a defensive Will all we're working for? God Himself is asking us to think about something more important than who gets our Rolex.

Have we gotten it through our heads that we're out of here before we know it? Have we ever given a thought to tomorrow, ultimately? Do we board a boat? Is crossing the channel like changing the channel? I heard of a man who actually thought death would make an exception in his case. A man? We all do. We can't believe we're terminal. Monks in Medieval time slept in coffins and addressed each other, not saying "good morning" until they said something like Chief Dan George in the classic movie *Little Big Man,* "It's a good day to die." The parable emphasizes the imminence of our departure. Today's the day the wise live for all it's worth, but with their "bags" packed. To others, "You fool, this night . . . ."

Obviously there is no future for a fool. Our earthly life is a planned obsolescence. The baby is born perfectly self-centered, which is as it should be, but for the baby to continue as a baby until he becomes a "big baby" is sick. The big baby is a fool.

The best literary example of a fool, carrying on the infantile self-absorption of a big baby is Ebenezer Scrooge, in Charles Dickens's, *A Christmas Carol.* Scrooge is not simply in

---

[13] Ibid, *Through Peasant Eyes,* pg. 66.
[14] Ibid, *Through Peasant Eyes,* pg. 67.

David A. Redding

the counting house; he's a monetary holding tank, perpetually counting up what's coming to him. Christmas is "humbug" to him, and the idea of sharing it is preposterous. Bob Cratchet, his workhorse, has been treated like one. And no fool is ever going to be anything other than a deposit box without going through hell.

So one Christmas Eve Scrooge goes through Hell. His first visitor that night of nightmares is a resident from there, Jacob Marley, his late partner, manacled, tortured, and shrieking exposure to that brutal existence, and the announcement that Scrooge was on the list. This, plus the visit of three heart-wrenching ghosts, effected Scrooge's rebirth.

The fool, in this parable, is not damned for his Godlessness, but for his unneighborliness. So far as this parable goes, a fool is someone who not only thinks what he has is all his; he won't share it.

A fool is not dumb; he's perverted. Greed has victimized him. He cannot come out and play by someone else. He can only play with himself. For an adult to be unable to share is to break the second part of the Great Commandment. The man is a fool because he's a tightwad. He is handcuffed as surely as the monkey who will not unclench his fistful of nuts in order to remove his paw from the jar. The fool who tries to take it all with him will take himself with it instead.

Jesus looked upon the rich young ruler, and tried to stop life from making a monkey of him. Jesus prescribed, "'Go sell what you possess and give it to the poor, and you will have treasure in Heaven; and come follow me.' When the young man heard this he went away sorrowful, for he had great possessions." (Matthew 19, 21, 22) Then Jesus explained, "It is easier for a camel to go through the eye of a needle than for a rich man to enter the Kingdom of God." (Matthew 19:24).

It's not easy for a fool to wise up, and we're all easily fooled. We think these verses apply to those who have more than we do, just as Carnegie could have referred this to Rockefeller. But most of us Americans have "great possessions" compared to Jesus who "had no place to lay his head," and only left a robe and perhaps sandals for the soldiers to gamble over.

We don't have to be rich to be fools over money. This parable is for our benefit, not simply for those in a higher bracket.

He Never Spoke without a Parable

The most powerful incident in the Gospel of a fool becoming wise is the account about Zacchaeus, the tax collector. Tax collectors not only collaborated with the Roman army of occupation, they were notoriously rich from corruption, as obnoxious as any mafia.

Zacchaeus, whose yard was no doubt full of rocks because of the hatred of the natives, became fascinated by Jesus. Since he was short of stature, he climbed a sycamore to see Jesus over the heads of the crowd the day He was in town.

Watching for Jesus is not safe for a fool, for Jesus saw him, called him by name, and invited Himself to the house of Zacchaeus for dinner, fatal for a fool. Being with Jesus broke Zacchaeus open, "Half of all I have I give to the poor, and I'll pay back those I've cheated four times over." Jesus declared, "Today, salvation has come to this house." Jesus not only saved bad men, he saved fools. (Luke 19:1-10).

David A. Redding

Jesus'
parables
make us
laugh
and cry
enough
to change
our
ways.

HE NEVER SPOKE WITHOUT A PARABLE
VOLUME FIVE: IT'S UP TO YOU

The parables
are not
so hard
to
understand
as they
are
to do.

He Never Spoke without a Parable

 CONTENTS

VOLUME V — IT'S UP TO YOU

1. The Brothers - Pro & Con – Matthew 21:28-32

    A Mustard Seed – Luke 13:18-19

    Yeast – Luke 13:20-22

2. Rustling up Dinner at Midnight – Luke 11:5:13

    A Widow Converted the Judge – Luke 18:1-8

3. Rich and Poor – Luke 16:19-31

4. The Rock – Luke 6:46-49

He Never Spoke without a Parable

THE BROTHERS: PRO & CON

What do you think about this father who had two sons? The father asked the first one, "My son, will you help me in our vineyard today?" He replied, "No." Later he went and helped. The father asked the second son the same. He said, "yes," but never did. Which one did his father's will? They all answered, "The first." And Jesus explained, "Even the Publicans and the harlots will get into the Kingdom before you ever do." "For John the Baptist showed you the way, and you didn't believe him, but the tax collectors and prostitutes believed. Even after you knew all this you still did not repent and come to believe in Him." Matthew 21:28-32

Paraphrased by the Author

Jesus weathered another scorching attack from religious authorities by telling this story about a father who asked his two sons to give him a day's work in his vineyard. One boy said, "yes" and one boy said, "no."

Naturally, we immediately take to the congenial son who responds respectfully to his father, and we are turned off by the boy who objected.

This parable takes off in an unexpected direction. The son who said "yes," never showed up. He was only talking through his hat. Jesus unmasks him as the juvenile delinquent. His sweet talk is simply part of his disguise, for that boy wouldn't lift a finger.

Jesus told this parable on these "church" people who were giving him such a hard time. The trouble with religion, Jesus is saying, is its "yes men." God's worst enemy is not the atheist, but these "promise breakers." God's opponents are not outside the synagogue throwing rocks, they are sitting inside splitting hairs.

He Never Spoke without a Parable

If you want to know why they killed Christ, all you need to do is read this parable. The prophets were stoned to death for verbally disemboweling religious people like this, "You worship me with your lips but your hearts aren't in it." Black spirituals were also brave enough to sing, "Everybody talkin' about Heaven ain't a'goin' there." The church is dying, not from the awful things said about it, but from talking itself to death. Our sermons are more deadly than their potshots. Mr. Gallop declares that most Americans believe in God, but Jesus doesn't go by ballot, but by obedience. When someone says they really want to get into God, we can sidetrack them with Bible study. So the church crumbles from an articulate but inactive clergy.

These two sons are all God has, and the first one is this "yessiree Bob" who goes up and down with the prayers, familiar with all the verses. He's a Christian recorder planted in what used to be called the "Amen corner." No terrorist, nor Muslim enslaving or killing Christians in the Sudan does a fraction of the harm done by hypocrites like this nodding boy. Did you ever read where Jesus was big on crime and addiction? No, His major opponent was on the jury and on the bench.

And Jesus tossed this accusation into the nest of those number one sons who excelled at public prayers, but wouldn't spit on you if you were on fire. These holy Joe's enraged Jesus, so he cannonaded them in this parable, "Criminals and call girls are going to beat you to Heaven." Jesus never condemned the whorehouse. What made him sick were those who turned religion into a theatre.

No one questions the preponderance of hypocrites, but did you ever run into anyone who admitted he was one? One hypocrite was exposed when he said he'd never join church because of all those hypocrites. The minister answered correctly, "We could always use one more." But the minister might have added, "I happen to be one myself." You can't miss meeting a hypocrite; he's in your mirror.

The son who says, "No, I won't go," is the hero in this story. What a psychologist Jesus was! Our "yes" means nothing if we have always been afraid or too slick to say "no." A child must not be denied the right to say "no." Only the ability to say "No" can nurture a solid "Yes."

My wife protected our sons' right to say "no" to me when the Beatle's long hair style erupted in teenagers in the sixties. It scandalized me with my proper Navy crew cut. I remember passing diplomas to our kindergartners at their commencement. A little guy came by as unshorn as Sampson. In my Navy barbers rank just below Admirals. Wild hair was not simply savage; it

He Never Spoke without a Parable

was a sin. You couldn't find this young graduate's face for the foliage. I said to the little Tumble Weed, "Son, who cuts your hair?" A hand reached out from under the canopy to push it aside enough for him to look up at me through his vines, "Ah, Dad, you know. Mom does."

Dee and I had it out that night. I finally noticed that the older boys obviously enjoyed the same cosmetologist. I kicked off, "When did we decide to do these hedge hog hairdos?" She let me have it. "They're doing O.K. in school aren't they?" "Yeah." "They're going to church aren't they?" "Yeah." "They're coming in at night O.K." "Yeah." "Well, can't they disagree with you about anything?" "Yeah."

As difficult as it is for parents, we must preside graciously over the liquidation of our domestic empire. Children must be taught to mind early on, then we must know when to abdicate the throne, finally resigning the presidency, to avoid a civil war or their elopement. My father used to quote to me John the Baptist's words to Christ, "You must increase, I must decrease." The best parents of little tots must decrease to remain good parents.

One of our eight year olds hated his cousin's hand me downs. He refused to wear them to church next door, so Dee decided to "decrease" but not disappear. She laid out three possible outfits on his bed and said, "I'm leaving for church. It would be best if you join me soon in one of these." He did.

One granddaughter was named Alicia Mae whom we soon nicknamed Alicia May-Not. Of course, complete submission to her was not permissible, but deserved appropriate respect. The entrance of her tricky negative was simply a sign that dad's dictatorship was doomed, and a more popular government was in order with some multiple-choice. God seemed to gravitate to the "no people" in the Bible. Moses objected when God tapped him, "I stutter, try Aaron." God liked honesty. Then Moses took God seriously, and when Moses came round it was not just good manners; it was enough of a resounding "yes" to cross the Red Sea.

Thomas told the other disciples that he would never believe Christ rose from the dead unless he could personally touch the nail holes in Jesus' hands and thrust his hand into Christ's spear wound, Christ welcomed that challenge, then Thomas jumped "in" with both feet, "My Lord and my God."

At twelve years Christ left his parents without permission for three days when He was found his mother scolded him for worrying them to death. In Luke two she complained! "We've been looking for you everywhere." Jesus did not apologize, and they did not unman him. No overkill. They respected his difference of opinion, and Mary and Joseph handled his "no" with great restraint. Jesus then went home under their authority, but with the stature of an older child, signified by a son's sitting on the men's side of the synagogue after his *bar mitzvah*.

We remember one prominent American for his heyday of saying "no;" but it prepped him for a great "yes" to God. It was Andrew Jackson! Unfortunately they've taken all the "no" out of his picture on the new twenty dollar bill, making him look almost as bland as Ben Franklin. Jackson, on the contrary, was in "no man's land" long enough to know how to qualify for "yes."

Jackson's approved biography from his official heirs, who supervise his historic Hermitage in Nashville, is by R.V. Reminis. But I quote here from Marvin Olasky, Editor, *World Magazine,* who praises Jackson's courage to stand up and say "no" to individual bullies as well as England. Rough as he was Jackson never broke his promises, and violent as he could be he said the strongest "yes" to God that ever came out of the White House. Lincoln, whom we revere, barely got elected, Washington had his foes, but this country went mad over Jackson. The people adored him. If you wanted anything done, get Jackson to back it. Count the cities and counties named for him. He was the most Republican Democrat.

Briefly, Jackson was born in 1767, educated at a Presbyterian school, and married in 1791, when he was twenty-four. By 1800 he settled down as a judge in Nashville, ran businesses, raced horses, and read the Bible regularly with his wife, Rachael.

The biggest bully in Tennessee in 1806 was named Charles Dickinson. He was a bully because he was the best marksman with a pistol in the entire State. Dickinson fought duels with anyone he opposed, either politically or socially. He usually killed his opponent.

When Dickinson, made a deliberate attempt to get Jackson into a duel and get rid of him, he insulted Jackson's wife, Rachael. Jackson's friends told him, "Don't duel with him. He's going to kill you." Jackson said, "Someone has to stand up to Dickinson; I will do it." Dickinson used to line up his shot by looking at the buttons on his opponent's coat. Jackson got an especially long loose coat and then he removed the buttons and sewed them back on three inches below the normal position. Since the buttons were changed, the bullet from Dickinson's shot missed Jackson's heart by about a quarter of an inch. It broke two ribs and lodged in Jackson's chest cavity, and would cause him problems the rest of his long life. Jackson steadied himself after taking that bullet, he aimed and he shot, not entirely straight, it was lower than Jackson intended, but the bullet in

God's providence ripped through Dickinson's intestines and Dickinson died.

Jackson became a living legend in Tennessee. In 1814 he led American volunteers in the defense of New Orleans against topnotch British regulars. These were the best professional soldiers in the world, the victors over Napoleon. Jackson's frontiersmen were close to panic. There was no way that these American volunteers could beat the British regulars. But Jackson did two things. First, he talked with his men about God's sovereignty, how God was in charge of battles and everything else in life. And then secondly he enlisted men that other generals would not touch. He brought in black soldiers and made sure they were paid, which was a "first." He brought in pirates, led by Jean Lafitte. Jean Lafitte was part Haitian, part Jewish, and according to reputation, trouble. Jackson talked to Lafitte and found that Lafitte really wanted, after being a pirate all those years, wanted a home. He wanted citizenship. He wanted to be an American. Jackson honored that desire.

So there was prayer, there was faith, there were extra soldiers from despised races and backgrounds, there were cannons that the pirates brought along. London's best soldiers, the best in the world, were left with 700 dead and twice that number wounded. American losses were seven killed, six wounded. You can imagine how sensational was the news of Jackson's victory, a very important victory. The British were not known for giving up territory. They would have held on to New Orleans, adjusting Washington's peace treaty. It would have changed the whole future course of American history.

Jackson publicly and frequently gave the glory to God for that battle climaxing the War of 1812. Jackson kept reading the Bible, started attending church regularly and praying with his wife. He invited evangelists to his home, the Hermitage in Nashville, so he could learn from them. Jackson's interest in Christ sometimes surprised people who knew him only by his dueling and his military reputation.

In 1816 there was a famous evangelist, Peter Cartwright, who was preaching in Nashville. There was a local pastor named Brother Mac who pulled Cartwright aside just before the service. Brother Mac said excitedly, "General Jackson is coming!" Cartwright knew about Jackson, but he was so irritated at this emphasis that he said loudly, "Who is General Jackson? If he don't get his soul converted, God will damn him!" After the service, Brother Mac hurried over to Jackson to apologize for Cartwright's remarks, but Jackson faced Cartwright and said, "You are a man after my own heart. I was very much surprised at Mr. Mac to think he would suppose that I would be offended at you. No sir, I told him that I highly approved of your independence. I told him that a minister of Jesus Christ ought to fear no mortal man.

Cartwright became a friend. He and Jackson met often and Jackson told him of his conversion. Cartwright later wrote an interesting memo in which he told of how he was once eating dinner with Jackson when there was a lawyer at the table, a newcomer to town who did not know about Jackson's religious beliefs. The lawyer started to make fun of Cartwright's evangelical beliefs. Cartwright responded very patiently, but Andrew Jackson sometimes did not have patience. "I saw," to quote Cartwright, "General Jackson's eyes strike fire as he sat by and heard the thrust made at the Christian religion."

The conversation became more intense when the lawyer asked, "Mr. Cartwright, do you believe there's such a place as hell, as a place of torment?" Cartwright said, "Yes." The lawyer responded, "I thank God I have too much good sense to believe any such thing." Jackson at that point could not hold his tongue. He said heatedly, "I thank God that there is such a place of torment as Hell." The lawyer then earned his spot in the Hall of Fame for dumb questions by asking, "General Jackson, what do you want with such a place of torment as Hell?" Jackson responded, "To put anti-Christian rascals like you in." According to Cartwright's story, the lawyer fled the room.

Jackson showed courage in an even tougher personal situation in 1820, just after he was elected to the Presidency at age 61. Rachael, his wife of thirty-seven years died. Some people, even those with strong belief could fall into a rage against God when a husband or wife dies. Jackson wrote, "We who are frequently visited by this chastening rod have the consolation to read in the Scriptures that whomever He chastens He loves and does it to make them mindful that this earth is not our abiding place."

Read Jackson's personal letters, and the notes of his personal secretary. One finds a Jackson whose faith was deepening. He is starting to think not about his own glory, not about the national glory, but primarily, about God's glory. He wrote that God afflicts us to discipline us for work in this life to prepare us for a better world. His faith deepened. One night, Jackson's personal secretary, Nicolas Tryst, needed guidance for a letter. Tryst knocked at Jackson's bedroom door and Jackson said "Come in," Tryst found Jackson partly undressed, sitting at a table reading his three nightly chapters of Scripture.

The most dramatic incident of his Presidency was the battle over the Second Bank of the

United States, partly federal, a complete monopoly. All deposits drew no interest. Daniel Webster and Henry Clay enjoyed its favoritism. Nicholas Biddle, the mighty Scrooge that ran this octopus, manipulated its control to squeeze the people until they screamed, but Jackson did not rule by statistics. He announced that banks should be private and competitive, "Until I can strangle this hydra of corruption, the bank, I will not shrink from my duty." "Regardless of all the clamor, I will do what is just and right. Biblically, this bank is wrong. It is forcing people to bow the knee to a golden calf."

In the middle of this crisis he was writing a letter to a friend on a Sunday morning about it, then interrupted himself. "I must stop. The church bells are ringing and I must attend."

That is how Jackson got through it, not reading the statistics, but reading the Scripture. And the people finally loved him for it far more than they ever loved any other President.

Remember, Jesus, distinguishing between the two boys, asked, "Which one did his father's will?" Not which one kept the commandments, not which one attended church, but beyond that, all the way to Gethsemane that night when Christ sweat blood over it, "Not my will, but Thine be done." One can keep the commandments, profess Christ, and still have to have his own way. Like Jackson, the boy that Jesus praised that day said, "No," loud and clear, but then went and did what his dad said. On the day the forgotten hero of New Orleans died, June 8, 1845, "He pointed to the Bible on the table by the bed and said, "That book is the rock upon which our republic rests. I hope to meet you all in Heaven, both white and black."

2
 **RUSTLING UP DINNER AT MIDNIGHT**

Which one of you would go to a friend's house at midnight to request, "Friend, lend me three loaves, for a friend of mine has arrived unexpectedly from a long trip, and I don't have a thing in the house to feed him."

The friend answers from inside, "Don't bother me. I have locked the door and the children are finally asleep in bed beside me. I cannot get up now to get you anything.

Even though he will not get up and give you anything because he is his friend, he will get up and give him whatever he wants because of his persistence. Don't you see? You will get what you ask for. You will find what you are looking for. The door will open at your knock.

For where's the father who would give his son a stone if he pled for bread? Or would hand him a snake if he asked for a fish? Or would give him a Scorpion if he begged for an egg!

So if you, limited as you are, know how to give good gifts to your children, how much more will your Father come personally to whoever asks? Luke 11:5-13

 **A WIDOW CONVERTED THE JUDGE**

He also told them a parable, so they would always pray and not lose heart. There was a heartless city judge who was had no respect for man or God. But a widow in his bailiwick kept pestering him to help her against her adversary. For a long time he refused, but finally she got to him and he told himself: "Though I could not care less about God and man, yet because this widow is driving me crazy, I will see that she gets justice.

So would not God look after his followers who cry night and day to him? I tell you He'll be quick about it. However, when I come back, will I find faith on earth?" Luke 18:1-8

Jesus' prayer life astounded his disciples! They knew that's how he whipped the Devil in that forty day marathon in the wilderness, and Jesus had also explained that a boy's impossible healing couldn't be done except by prayer, and, as the King James adds, "fasting." So that time he went up the mountain alone to pray all night was no surprise. Without prayer, we can't have forgiveness and without forgiveness we're dead.

Prayer not only ignites His ministry, and our life. It is what Jesus did when he was desperate in the end at Gethsemane, when He repeatedly begged the Three to pray for Him before He went off alone and flung Himself, His face to the ground, until Luke said He sweat blood.

Long before these final prayers the disciples demanded Jesus share this secret, "Lord, teach us to pray." He not only answered them immediately with "the Lord's Prayer," He illustrated why they couldn't quit. Jesus said, suppose you had unexpected company late some night, not so unusual, for in the desert it was often too hot to travel in the daytime. This visitor happens to catch you without a bite to eat in the house, so you run next door, to obtain the ingredients for the meal, probably shouting, instead of knocking, so he knows you're friendly. Jeremais and Bailey disagree whether the woman of the house bakes for the day or the week, but agree that the village always knows who has some left over.

Implicit in the story is Jesus' affection and amusement for the way they lived life there. Then Jesus' story throws one for a loop. The response from inside is not only unfriendly; he hisses back that he's not getting up for anybody. The kids are all tucked in beside him, no doubt on the floor mat in their one room houses, having gotten their last cup of water. Our authorities quarrel whether the sliding lock that bars the door would also wake the dead, but whatever, the answer's "no." This sleepy head's refusal is unthinkable. These people would die before refusing legendary hospitality, no matter how ungodly the hour. So since this neighbor cannot be shamed into supplying the three loaves, the petitioner hangs in there until the bread comes out the window. Dr. Bailey may be mistaken to play down the persistence that the parable features. Even the modern New Testament from Jesus' native Aramaic plays up persistence, emphatically, all the more in the face of such shameful inhospitality.[1]

    However, though this grouchy Grinch will not get out of bed because you are a friend of his and supposed to help even a hungry enemy, he will do it to get rid of a headache. And if he will help you, if you keep after him, don't you think Almighty God would too? "Ask, and the gift will be yours, seek and you will find, knock and the door will open to you!"

    Jesus caps this off by another powerful persuader, "If your son cried for bread, would you pass him a stone? If he begged for meat, would you offer snake? Or if he were hungry for an egg until he could taste it, would you sting him with a Scorpion? Well, if you, limited as you are, would go out of your way for your children, how much more will your Heavenly Father give even the Holy Spirit from Heaven to those who ask Him?" Would we be better at this than God?

    Jesus enforces our praying until Kingdom Come by a second parable of a young widow who kept pestering a heartless Judge who couldn't care for God, or anybody else. The two parables are obvious twins, for both petitioners go for help to people who could care less, underlining Jesus' idea that if scoundrels can't resist determined pests, how can you believe God can? This woman kept fussing at this Judge until he yelled "Uncle!" It can practically be translated, "She's about to strangle me with her everlasting nagging." Like the neighbor, the hardboiled judge too did what the widow asked, not because he had a change of heart, but because he couldn't take it anymore. So if you can get help barking up the wrong tree, what about asking the one who loves you most? The time comes of course, when we must stop praying but not until we have prayed "all out."

    Jesus poured almost obsessive determination into these two parables, turning prayer into a full time job, as though, as Dr. George Buttrick said, "Heaven's determined not to hear what we're

---

[1] George M. Lamsa. Trans. Devorus Publication, 1933, P.O. Box 550, Marina Del Rey, CA   90294.

He Never Spoke without a Parable

not determined it shall hear." If we can't even remember what we prayed for last Sunday, and never prayed for the same thing two weeks in a row, that wasn't prayer, it was a joke. Prayer is the way NBA superstars like Stockton and Malone handled overtime. All these casual, "God bless you's" that preachers sprinkle in their conversation have nothing to do with prayer. The ritual mutterings the mob makes, when it spurts into the cathedral Sunday's chattering to God while staring at the woman's hair in front of them make prayer tomfoolery. God doesn't bother with such third class mail. Anyone who assumes one outburst to God's enough makes prayer a pity.

That night when Jacob was praying within an inch of his life, and finally bumped into an angel, he didn't say, "excuse me." He grabbed him and hung on for such dear life, the powerful Being finally submitted, "Let go of me!" And Jacob didn't say, "How about an appointment early next week?" Jacob panted, "I'm not letting go until you bless me!" So the angel did what he wouldn't have done if Jacob hadn't maxed out. You know why Jacob limped ever after? It's where the angel struck him. Jacob prayed so hard he sprained his leg. Have we ever prayed that hard? Prayer meetings died because they weren't praying, they were playing.

Why does God do this to us? It's to show us He's God, and not Santa Claus. Prayer's not a push button, as your fortune pops out of a ten-cent machine. The idea that God knows, and we don't, He can and we can't, sinks in slowly.

Prayer's an education in humility. "They that wait upon the Lord," not those who make God wait, "they that wait upon the Lord, shall mount up with wings as eagles," they shall run, and never run down.

Thank God, we don't get too prompt prayer service. There are so many prayers we should never have made. Thank God we didn't always get what we asked for. One fellow indefatigably prayed for the wrong thing in the Old Testament; he wouldn't let go. And he got it. The Bible reports that God shriveled him.

So pray, for Christ's sake, and if your prayer continues to be marinated in His Spirit, soaking up His light, it will turn into the right prayer. The longer we pray beneath the Cross, the quicker our cheap prayers will fall off.

Galileo made a pilgrimage to the tomb of St. Anthony to pray for money, for health for his children, and for his aged mother. But while kneeling by the tomb of the blessed St Anthony, for whom how many hospitals and schools are named, pondering the sacrifice Anthony made of wife, and family, Galileo found himself praying a far different prayer than he'd started out to make, "I beg you, St. Anthony, to intercede for me with Jesus Christ, that He should enlighten my mind and let me invent something great to further human knowledge." "So would God not look after His followers who cry night and day to Him?"

I can't remember when I did not yearn to be a writer. And I was on my way, and finally into The Graduate School of English. The guy who studied with me shared my passion to publish books, and we were concentrating on Mark Twain and Emily Dickinson. My grades maintained my graduate school standing, but something happened to me that made me leave English for Divinity, though my father advised against it, as I unsuccessfully discouraged my children. But while I believe God practically forced me to do it, I knew it was right for me.

What nearly broke my heart was I thought I had to give up the writing. My beautiful wife Dee, was much more than a wife to me and mother to our family, which included more than she bore. She saw me working hard on my sermons and struggling to acknowledge my identity as a minister, and I still hate that word, "Reverend." I finally came up with a sermon on the Lord's Prayer that didn't put her to sleep. So she said she was going to send it off to the *Reader's Digest*. They sent back a pink slip, "This is not suitable for our editorial needs." She kept sending it to other periodicals. Same thing. Someday I'll shoot the editor who came up with that phrase. She didn't send it to any religious magazine. I'd have died first. The big magazine then was *Life Magazine*, a weekly. She sent it there, for their editorial. They did manage a personal rebuke, "We are able to write our own editorials." She sent it back to their Chief Editorial Writer. Didn't I tell you persistence may be pathological? We were also praying for $750 to start building a cabin in a little woods my Dad and I had.

I was sitting in the library of the University of Cincinnati where I taught surrounded by those signs of "Silence." Over the loud speaker I thought I heard, "Mr. Redding, come to the main desk for a long distance call." The voice on the other end solemnly intoned, "Mr. Redding, we want to use your piece on The Lord's Prayer as our *Life Magazine* Easter editorial. Would $750 be acceptable?" I finally choked out, "I thought it would." The *Reader's Digest* picked it up from there. Publishers then came to me for twenty some books over the years. Jesus let me ride into writing on His own Prayer. That, and a little wifely persistence.

He Never Spoke without a Parable

3
 # RICH MAN, POOR MAN

A rich man wore expensive Phoenician purple, fine linen underwear imported from Egypt, and feasted sumptuously everyday. A poor wretch named Lazarus covered with boils,[2] was left at the rich man's door. He yearned to eat the scraps that fell from the rich man's table. Dogs came and licked the poor man's oozing sores.

When the poor man died, the angels carried him to the arms of another rich man named Abraham. The rich man also died, and they buried him. While he was suffering Hell's torment he looked up and saw Abraham holding Lazarus in the distance. So he shouted, "O my father Abraham, have mercy on me and send Lazarus to dip his finger in water and wet my burning tongue."

Abraham replied, "My son, you had your pleasures while Lazarus suffered, now it is the other way around; besides there is a great abyss between us and you, and no way to cross over. "Then, O my Father, send him back to my father's house to warn my five brothers so they won't have to come to Hell." Abraham answered, "They have Moses and the prophets. That's enough." No, Father Abraham, they will repent if only someone from the dead would talk to them." "No, if they won't listen to Moses and the Prophets, they won't pay any attention to someone who came back from the dead." Luke 16:19-31

---

[2] The modern *New Testament from the Aramaic* uses the translation "boils."

Jesus puts His unique spin on an old fable the Jews brought back from Egypt over a thousand years before. It is about a rich man and a poor man who were switched in the next world. Only Luke discovered this masterpiece! You can't miss Jesus' "rich man." He is dressed to kill in a magnificent mantle of wool in costly Phoenician purple, and wearing expensive linen underwear imported from Egypt. He doesn't do anything except feast sumptuously all day long. Jesus didn't name him, but Jerome translated the word rich, into Latin as "Dives" when he translated the vulgate, which Catholics have used since 600 A.D. So everyone has called him Dives ever since. Dives was no scoundrel, he was simply a gorgeous eating and drinking machine.

Jesus' poor man is dying! He is the only character Jesus ever named in all his parables. Lazarus! He may be a paraplegic for it says he "lay;" the Greek means he was "flung" at Dive's door. That's not all. He was covered with boils that must have hurt and stunk to Heaven, except for the dogs' compassionately licking them in lieu of the questionable malpractice of current dermatology.

While this is Jesus' only reference to dogs, it is most appreciative. These dogs were the only friends that Lazarus had. Lazarus lived a dog's life. Archaeologists have excavated their well-kept graveyards from that period. They were memorialized in those days as much for nursing as for guarding.

Lazarus fights beside these dogs for whatever falls from Dive's groaning table, which was far more that crumbs. Bread was used instead of silverware to dip into the dinner bowls back then. Bread was also the napkin for the well fed. So enough dunked morsels found their way to Lazarus to keep him alive, perhaps served partly by friendly retrievers. But while Dives was dying from fat, Lazarus was dying for it.

The name, Lazarus, means "God helps," and did He ever help Jesus raise his friend, Lazarus, from the dead. Whether that miracle took place before or after Jesus made up this story, it adds to its poignancy. The name, Lazarus, has still held up, even in our market place, but we will certainly never forget fancy Dives dining at the table and under it Lazarus groaning among the growling dogs.

In the next scene, Jesus pictures them in the next world, something he never did before or since. Lazarus had probably been shoveled into a cart after his last banquet, but Jesus reported that angels came for Lazarus and lovingly escorted him personally to the bosom of Abraham, meaning, "What more could you ask?" And isn't it dramatic to run into Abraham there, particularly in this parable, for Abraham had also been a very rich man, so could certainly understand Dives if anyone could.

What an eye opener! Christians generally assume that the only way you can get into Heaven is either by being good or confessing Christ, but the only celestial credentials Lazarus possessed was his poverty and the devastating bone and skin diseases that crippled and killed him; he won handicap parking above.

According to Jesus' story, the next world was waiting with its emergency vehicles for the arrival of earth's severely injured. Lazarus not only ends up in I.C.U., the best box seat's reserved, not only beside but embraced by the Founder and Father of the Hebrew people, illustrating Jesus' words, "The first shall be last, and the last, first."

Jesus looks after God's reputation here, for as hard as it is to suffer Hell on earth, "The crooked will be made straight," and God's going to make it up to those who never got a break. "Rich man, poor man's" an astonishing demonstration of Jesus' beatitudes in Luke:

> *O how happy you poverty stricken wretches will be, for you are awarded God's kingdom. O how happy are all those who are starving, for you will be fed, bountifully. And O how happy will be those I hear crying now, for your time is coming soon to laugh with joy.* Luke 6:20-22

Critics may scorn Jesus' promises of the future as "pie in the sky," and this doesn't excuse our not pitching in today, but this parable and Jesus' beatitudes, are the Word of God to those who have been abandoned. Earth may fail Lazarus; Heaven will not.

It says Dives was buried, it doesn't say Lazarus was. But despite Dive's big funeral it doesn't take Dives long to discover he's in trouble. He arrived over there, of course, before St. Peter, but the story borrows the already popular concept that Dives went to Hell. Dives may have been unable to push himself back from the table on earth, but Hell immediately did it for him, though he was stretching the patience of the Chief Justice, by assuming he still qualified for negotiations. He was encouraged in that hope because he could see Abraham and Lazarus luxuriating in the distance. Dives still thinks he has enough clout with his own father Abraham to order Lazarus into bringing him at least a wet finger to cool his burning tongue, a modest request for such a greedy bully. Jesus' parable certifies life after death, advance notice of the survival of personality in the next world. Dives immediately recognized both Lazarus and Abraham, and obviously they had no trouble hearing Hell from there, particularly in the lobby of those awesome kingdoms where this parable leaves us.

People have recently shared with me dreams and visitations that suggest a conjunction of these three kingdoms upon someone's departure. A bluebird displayed itself prominently to a loved one in an unlikely place shortly after a lover of bluebirds died. The viewer scorned the word "coincidence." She wept with joy upon the arrival of such a reassuring messenger. And here is Jesus' parable letting us in on a conversation from earth while apparently Heaven and Hell intersect.

Jesus is definitely not saying that you are going to Hell if you're loaded, and going to Heaven if you're down on your luck, but the parable is implying there will be an audit, punishing the cold blooded and rewarding uncomplaining victims. The parable is not preaching that Hell is in concrete, nor that Heaven is automatic.

Any hope for Dives is still remote, for he is not yet near repentance. He's too busy dealing with his dehydration. In fact Abraham reminds Dives that he had it good, and yet he was not any good to Lazarus. So now Lazarus is comfortable and Dives is not. Besides, as Abraham explains, between them yawns a Grand Canyon of difference preventing contact between the two.

Dives could not help but be thrilled by Abraham's calling him, "my son." That certainly does not sound like an exasperated Jewish father about to tear up his will and obliterate his son's name forever.

Dives still cannot get it through his head that the game is over, that he has already had his reward, so Dives comes up with a second errand for Lazarus to run. Though Dive's punishment is obviously begun, Dives still has Abraham's ear, much as our cartoons speculate we would have St. Peter's. Now Dives wants Lazarus to go warn his five brothers of this wretched address. Dives' rough therapy seems to be working. At least it has gotten Dives' mind off himself. He may be sluggish, but suddenly he's eager to do a good turn for his kid brothers, something that would never have occurred to most of us in such excruciating circumstances.

Isn't this where Charles Dickens got the idea in his Christmas Carol of permitting the late Jacob Marley to return from the inferno, and nightmare Ebenezer Scrooge with such a rattle of chains and throat clearing that it will terrify that old skinflint into changing before it's too late?

Abraham doesn't let up. Dives is thinking fast and plays his last card and goes down fighting. It is fascinating that Jesus does not portray desperate Dives as hysterical or vicious. Obviously Dives flunked earth, but for someone who's in the pit, which surely would squeeze out one's true colors, Hell may be excavating an admirable quality in this bloated glutton, whom I am beginning to realize is not so distant a cousin of mine.

Abraham calmly tells Dives what he no doubt knew, that ringing Hell's bells again was a waste of time on his brothers, "Determined unbelievers are not going to believe even if someone rose from the dead."

Hell is jammed, according to Jesus' parables, not so much by thieves and murderers, but by respectable people like Dives, and the man God called a fool, who was not at fault so much as guilty of default. Lazarus starved and suffered underfoot while Dives ate his way through it.

Discussions take place about which of our Presidents were Christians. Some question Jefferson's Orthodoxy, others remember McKinley repeating the Lord's Prayer as he died, and Jackson was certainly redemptively immersed in the Bible despite his proclivity for dueling.

But in light of this parable, an incident comes back to me from the boyhood of Abraham Lincoln. It comes from Volume V of Carl Sandburg's *Abraham Lincoln*. Something like this boy's heartfelt sharing was what Dives was missing. Lincoln reminisced:

> The rare treat when I was a boy was when my mother found some ginger and made gingerbread men. I could tell from the smells from the oven that they were underway one day so I stayed nearby. She gave me three, and I went under a nearby hickory to sit down and eat them. Just then the boy next door showed up and sat down beside me. His family was even poorer then mine. Pretty soon he said, "Abe, gimme a man." So I gave him one. He had his down by the time I had the head off mine. Then he said, "Abe, give me that other'n," so I gave it to him, and it went down like the first. I said, "'Pears to me you like gingerbread men." "Abe," he sighed, "I don't suppose there's anybody on earth likes gingerbread men better'n I do, and gets less than I do."

Lincoln heard and blessed his Lazarus.

Is Dives done for? The old Dives is, but David sang in his Psalms, "Thou wilt not leave my soul in Hell." We cannot imagine Jesus doing anything that is not therapeutic. There is an abyss between someone imprisoned in himself like the Priest or Levite, and the Good Samaritan who was free to love and share. But wherever that torturous prison is punctured, there's Heaven with its joy. "With God nothing is impossible," and since Jesus is an expert with pardon, could he not build a bridge that might finally marry Heaven and Hell?

4
 THE ROCK

Everyone who listens to my words and does them is like someone who dug down to rock for the foundation to build his house. So it stood firm when the storm struck and flooded it because it was built on rock but he who hears me and does nothing about it, is like someone who built his house on sand, and it came down with a big crash in the storm. Luke 6:46-49

This parable was Jesus' benediction to his famous "Sermon on the Mount." And while it is not his last parable, its finality fits it for the ending to all His forty parables.

"Whoever ignores me," Jesus warns, "is a fool. He is like someone who built his house on sand."

Visiting St. Augustine Beach twenty years after I lived there, I found a block of houses tumbling into the surf. The old curator of the church I served there had once pointed to a piece of pipe sticking above the water about a hundred feet out to sea then said, "That's what is left of the backstop where we used to play ball forty years ago." Then as we drank coffee in my house on the waterway, he added, "You must not keep this house too long, because it was built on fill, for in your lifetime a hurricane will come in from the Atlantic and sweep it away."

I felt as though Jesus, who had constructed this parable from his own building experience, was speaking to me. I know He was those three nights of terror in the typhoon in the South Pacific, when the heightening seventy-five foot waves all but capsized my ship, the old *Saratoga* when I was in the Navy. Again, I got the message that anything short of something solid will not do for a foundation.

Jesus did not say that building on sand was sinful. He meant it was idiotic. Driving on the

He Never Spoke without a Parable

wrong side of the road at night in heavy traffic is not simply illegal, it is suicide. We could entitle Jesus' parable, "How not to be a fatality." This is not simply a helpful hint.

People like to put Jesus on remote, categorizing Him as a well-meaning moralist who had some good ideas to preserve and improve our quality of life. Hardly. Jesus died putting up these forty road signs, so we could make it without having a head-on collision. To dismiss Him simply as a great teacher is to sidestep Him. He is a lifeguard. He died to protect us against insanity.

So what are we finding under our house? You can tell by the calls we take that we can't wait to take somebody apart; but isn't that demolition instead of construction? Are my daydreams an unreliable building product or not? How much of my hard labor goes into nursing grievances? High profile religious types can wallow too long in pornographic fantasies and who of us has not had murder in his heart? None of our mental rubbish is sturdy enough to under-gird us. That is erecting sand castles in the air. A life built on and around such cheap shots, such sly underhandedness, is mushrooming us over a sinkhole.

When will I obey these parables I have written about? How many poor victims have we left by the roadside? All of the parables are construction manuals. Do our prayers imply we're better than those we pray for? Do we easily make promises to God we do not keep? Do we head toward the head tables unaware it is a dead end, stuffing under our "house" material that will rot, that won't sustain the structure of life?

Building on sand is not all bad; it is just not reliable. We may not be guilty of criminal activity, but leaning on misnamed securities. Profits are not pillars. Perhaps our nights are swallowed, not with plotting evil, just by filler. Even worse than battering rams, our underpinning is being softened up by incessant soap operas, or caving in from too many best sellers; maybe we have been hollowed out, not coming home drunk, but by just playing at everything, and not playing for keeps, until we're just putting in time, or killing time.

Or do we have too much of a good thing? The right amount of sand is required to make mortar hard as rock. Ty Cobb, the baseball sensation almost a century ago, indicted himself before he died as overdoing our beloved pastime, "You cannot eat baseball, and sleep baseball and study baseball year after year and just stop like that." A little solitaire might do a lot of us some good, but you can't expect a house of cards to stand. Remember when the wolf huffed and he puffed and he blew down the first little pig's house of straw?

"Therefore," Jesus announced, "whoever hears Me out and follows it up is like the wise carpenter who built his house upon a rock."

And Jesus, as gentle as He was, to say to the woman he saved from stoning: "Neither do I condemn you. You are free to go and sin no more." Jesus is hard as stone when it comes to stopping us when the bridge ahead is out. Who could be more tolerant: "He who is not against Me," Jesus explains, "is for Me," but when it comes to preventing us from self-destruction, He is ruthless: "Unless you forgive your brother from your heart, neither will I forgive you." Moses' commandments were tough, but not as ironclad as Jesus' ultimatums. These parables make you measure your life twice.

One of Jesus' stories was an invitation to go out to dinner, not simply with a king, but the King, "Are you coming to dinner with me or not?" Communion is both an option and a must. Go ahead! Eat, but how beautiful to share with the one who is under your table, as Lazarus was, as well as with God above.

The parables suggest we:

>stick up for the underdog,
>
>>choose a wallflower,
>>
>>>protect a child,
>>>
>>>>welcome a stranger,
>>>>
>>>>>help your neighbor out of their driveway.

It's what you call your foundation. Don't cheat. Sometime give up your seat, allow the car beside you to squeeze in, and park at the far end of the lot.

It is customary for all of us to busy ourselves with that part of the house that is above ground, what *shows*. We toss and turn over colors and furnishings and window dressings. We go at building backwards, beginning at the top down, from the outside in the wrong end first. Isn't that chandelier a knockout? But what's underfoot? The front door should embrace the visitor, but the threshold should support him. What's our place based on? Are we off base? Is it only a showplace? Is our faith a front or a footer? What will it take to topple any one of us?

I know someone whom disease could not knock down. Divorce couldn't do it. He lost his

He Never Spoke without a Parable

job. His savings were swept away, his partner took him for all he had. I couldn't believe he was still standing. I realized, finally, that he stood up under the worst that life could do to him because he was "standing on the promises," not on his own reputation.

Jesus has been left out of lives like the leaning tower of Pisa, but God made Him our Cornerstone. Who do you trust? CNN? The Almanac? I leaned too long on the complaints brought by Religion 101. Then I shifted my weight. Even that old skeptic playwright, George Bernard Shaw, surprised me, "I would sooner trust St. John," he said, "than all his scholarly commentators." Even though he wasn't perfect, President Andrew Jackson's last words were, pointing to the Bible open beside his bed, "That book is the rock on which our Republic rests." You and I must never stop singing, "On Christ the solid rock we stand, all other ground is sinking sand." "Who trusts in God's unchanging love, builds on the rock that naught can move."

CLOSING PRAYER

My closing prayer is adapted from the Dean of Cambridge University's address to the freshman convocation the year after the First World War ended, when so many of the students did not return. It was read in the film, *Chariots of Fire*, and perhaps these words will remind you of the many students who've gone before you, to make you safe and free to study and live. In the film the freshmen are all standing there in the refectory with all the empty seats beside them. (The boy in the room next to me my freshman year in college did not come back because he lost his life dragging his sergeant to safety.) The Dean had trouble speaking,

> *I take the war list, and as I run down it, name after name which I cannot read, which we, who are older than you cannot hear, without emotion. Names which are only names to you, to us they summon up face after face, full of honesty, goodness, and intellectual promise, the flower of a generation, the glory of our country, they died for her and all she stands for; and now by tragic necessity, their dreams become yours. For their sakes, let me persuade you to examine yourselves. Let each one discover where your true challenge of greatness lies, remember Christ's saying "He who would be the greatest of all, must be your servant." Seize it and rejoice in it and let no power on earth deter you from it, so help you God."*

He Never Spoke without a Parable

ABOUT THE AUTHOR

ditorials for *Life Magazine* and a feature he wrote for *Reader's Digest* plunged author David A. Redding into publishing twenty-five books. *He Never Spoke without a Parable* is his life's work. Harper and Row did well with his earlier work, *The Parables He Told*, in the late 1970's, but this latest, comprehensive rendition is far more entertaining and enriched with recent scholarship. Volumes I and II of this work were released in 2000 and 2001.

Dr. Redding has been the minister of the renowned Flagler Memorial Presbyterian Church in St. Augustine, Florida, and the celebrated Liberty Presbyterian Church, the Amish built timber frame cathedral in Delaware, Ohio. He is also treasured across the country as an inspiring speaker, and quoted in popular radio ministry programs and best-selling book collections of poignant stories. His preaching and writing are enhanced by his homespun, spellbinding, story telling ability. David is available for motivational conferences, spiritual retreats, and other speaking engagements on his website, www.davidredding.com.

David and his wife, Dorothy McCleery Redding, have eight children. Marion and David M. (Bobbie) are ministers. John (Shari) is a custom homebuilder who was the Construction Manager for Liberty's Barn Church. Mark (Sarah) is a pediatrician, and founder and Executive Director of the Community Health Access Project (C.H.A.P.). Rob (Pam) is a hotel executive, Chris (Pam) a restauranteur and Datil Do It Sauce inventor, Sandy (Fred) is an executive in health care and a wife, mother and grandmother extraordinaire, and Phûc is our Vietnamese businesswoman and cosmetic genius.

The family still gathers in the old stone house they built together on a farm by the Scioto River famous for Tecumseh.

NOTES

NOTES

NOTES

NOTES

NOTES

NOTES

NOTES

NOTES